TESTIMONIALS

"Dr. Gladys has written a must-read primer for today's leaders managing remote employees. She has infused humor and a dose of reality to a relevant and challenging topic facing virtual leaders. This book includes nuggets of intriguing facts that will help navigate the turbulent waters of virtual leadership. Read this book—and learn from one of the best!"

—Dr. Elizabeth S. Birch, PMP

"Take heed of Dr. Ann Gladys' invisible leadership model—it is a must for all organizations. As a veteran virtual employee, teleworking has provided longevity and happiness in my work-life balance. I cannot imagine a work environment without it: a benefit that rivals all others. Listen, Learn, Implement."

—Mimi Bruce, Contracts Specialist

"Dr. Ann Gladys answered my questions of *why* and *how* to lead virtual teams. In combining theory with practice in each chapter of her book, she created a simple yet comprehensive structure for navigating through the complexity of leading virtual teams."

—Kasia Fuiks, Ph.D., Assistant Department Chair

"The Invisible Leader " is ahead of the curve, defining changes in the modern work force. Dr. Gladys' book defines ways that will change the model for positive relationships between organizations and employees. With a passion to promote successful outcomes between employers and employees in the evolving digital world, Ann Gladys hits the mark!"

—*Anne Meridien, Chief of Staff,*
Pacific Grande Services

"Dr. Gladys examines and offers a compelling guide to one of the most prevailing topics in today's work environment, the Invisible Leader. This book is engaging, informative, and provides practical steps to successfully lead a virtual workforce."

—*Kim Pack, Vice President, Wolf Den Associates*

"Dr. Ann Gladys has a wealth of great advice that provides useful strategies for remote leadership. The concepts are clear and succinct and easily implemented. I highly recommend this book for organizations that need to train employees on reliable and proven virtual leadership tactics."

—*Dr. Lynn Pregitzer,*
Educational and Academic Thought Leader

"Finally a book that discusses invisible leadership in a way that's engaging and fun. Every company that has virtual employees should read this book to help guide their success in all areas that are important to their virtual employees."

—*Daveed Rangel,*
Investor / Real Estate Professional

"*The Invisible Leadership Model* is a "must read" for any leader or organization looking to enter into a Virtual Workplace environment. Dr. Gladys' experience and insightful anecdotes make this the ultimate guidebook for teleworking. Her common sense approach makes this book even more worthwhile. I highly commend Dr. Gladys for bringing this topic to the forefront in our global world."

—*David Shumway,*
Former Contracts Administrator

"Dr. Gladys has written an engaging and indispensable guide for leading remotely. It is a must read for remote leaders as the number of invisible employees rapidly increases."

—*Dr. Brenda Wilson,*
Founder/Owner of The Green Giraffe Consulting Group

THE INVISIBLE LEADER

The Model for Leading in the Virtual Workspace

Dr. Ann Gladys

Sommét Publishing

The Invisible Leader: The Model for Leading in the Virtual Workspace
Published by Sommét Publishing
Copyright © 2019 by Dr. Ann Gladys

All rights reserved.

Sommét Publishing
Address: 1199 Pacific Highway #2803
San Diego, CA 92101
Email: sommetpublishing@sommetenterprises.com
https://www.sommetenterprises.com/Somm-t-Publishing.html

Limit of Liability/Disclaimer of Warranty:

Publishing and editorial team: Author Bridge Media, www.AuthorBridgeMedia.com
Project Manager and Editorial Director: Helen Chang
Editor: Jenny Shipley
Publishing Manager: Laurie Aranda
Cover Design: Deb Tremper

Library of Congress Number: 2018914215

ISBN: 978-0-9600555-0-0 -- paperback
978-0-9600555-1-7 -- hardcover
978-0-9600555-2-4 -- ebook
978-0-9600555-3-1 -- audiobook

Ordering Information:

Quantity sales. Special discounts are available on quantity purchases by corporations, associations, and others. For details, contact the publisher at the address above.

Printed in United States of America.

DEDICATION

I dedicate this book to my children, Brett and Kelly. For way too many years with business and travel I was an invisible parent and here I am having written a book on invisible leadership. My children have always provided me the emotional and intellectual support to keep moving forward even when I thought I couldn't move another step in my personal development. They have listened to me whine. They have patted me on the back for each achievement. And they have called me out whenever I erred or waivered. I could not be more blessed for their patience and understanding. They are AMAZING and I thank God every day for blessing me with them.

Brett and Kelly, you are my everything!

CONTENTS

Part III
The How-To's of Becoming A Successful Invisible Leader

Part IV
The Final Takeaways

ACKNOWLEDGMENTS

I am continually grateful to my family and friends who have encouraged my progress in this journey to authorship. Their input and encouragement gave me suggestions and insights to take this project to completion.

In gratitude also to my wonderful doctoral professors at Pepperdine University, especially Farzin Madjidi who made each of my courses with him incredible, and my Dissertation Chair Dr. June Schmieder Chair of Leadership Studies at the Graduate school Education and Psychology. In addition to being an incredible inspiration, June introduced me to her SPELIT Model that I have used as a foundational element in building the Invisible Leadership Model.

Also, a very special shout-out to Author Bridge Media and Helen Chang and her team. In particular, to Jenny Shipley for helping to keep me driven and focused during my writing journey.

Many blessings to all of you.

DEFINING THE PROBLEM—
DESCRIBING THE JOURNEY

Is my organization working virtually,
or virtually working?

"We like to give people the freedom to work where they want,
safe in the knowledge that they have the drive and expertise to
perform excellently, whether they [are] at their desk
or in their kitchen.
Yours truly has never worked out of an office,
and never will."

—Richard Branson

Welcome to a journey that will take you from sleepless nights worrying about your business numbers to an incredibly successful virtual organization! But first, you may ask, what is a virtual organization? The answer is simple. A virtual organization is one where you are an invisible leader of invisible/remote employees with employees that you rarely see in person. Such an organization begs questions like. Do you lose sleep at night wondering if your remote staff is really working? Are your invisible employees just *phoning it in?* Are your "numbers" stagnate or, worse yet,

1

plummeting? If so, you have come to the right book! In fact, many virtual organizations fail! And where does the blame fall? You guessed it—to the captain of the ship, the invisible leader! This book is designed to solve and address your challenges in creating and sustaining a successful invisible organization. My promise to you is to make your sleepless nights disappear with business metrics that are better than ever! Believe me, I have lived the good, the bad, and the ugly sides of invisible leadership and, I too, have lost plenty of sleep. But there is a light at the end of the tunnel and it comes in the form of the Invisible Leadership Model grounded in transformational leadership!

Through some 30+ years of leadership experience, more than 20 years' experience in the arena of invisible leadership, and extensive doctoral research, I created an approach and a model so that you can achieve and sustain a successful invisible organization. This book offers a leadership assessment and a new Invisible Leadership Model. These tools give you the easiest and best ways to create an organization that has you counting money instead of sheep! This book also allows you to experience the stories, theories, and takeaways that will color your leadership tour in this book like tourist attractions on a vacation!

The book includes four parts, each containing important components. Part I delves into the invisible leader in you and offers food for thought concerning the definition of a successful virtual organization as well as insights into your personal leadership style. Part II addresses the dynamics of an invisible organization; social, political, economic, legal, intercultural, and technical. Part III gets into the "How-To's" of becoming a successful invisible leader through transformational leadership. And

Part IV provides the Invisible Leadership Model and an associated assessment. So let's get down to making you the most successful invisible leader ever! We will begin with a little background into the virtual leadership complex.

Over the past few years working virtually has become more commonplace than ever. Nevertheless, many managers and leaders are fundamentally averse to running an organization where their employees are not within arm's reach; leading some to question if the physical presence of employees is the executive's security blanket. So much of a leader's view of remote employees rests on the level of trust a manager has with employees as well as the manager's personal proclivity towards trust. And while one may argue that a leader's inclination towards trust is sufficient to guide the decision to permit employees to work at home (or any other off-site venue), there are economic factors that may also advance the decision to create a virtual organization.

It is important to note that an office that is physically available for use 168 hours a week but used perhaps eight to 16 hours per day is no longer financially viable. In fact, studies have shown that the annual foot print savings per teleworker can run $11,000 year on year. For a large corporation, this equates to $11M per year for 1,000 employees! Economic factors such as this, coupled with advances in technology, make the decision to employ remote workers difficult to ignore. Nonetheless, perturbations on the part of management related to trust continue to plague the path forward of the virtual workspace.

Losing visual contact with employees can create conditions tantamount to flying an airplane in the clouds with no visibility, only instrumentation. In this case, the pilot must navigate the skies with the belief that the instruments are functioning as promised. Just as the lack of visuals requires trust in the instruments, so too, the invisible leader must trust his/her virtual employees. Ultimately, the leader is left with a decision that rests on two questions: can I trust my employees, and can I afford not to trust my employees? A primary theme of this book is to examine a dilemma faced by many virtual leaders; a dilemma that poses the question "are my employees working virtually or virtually working?"

The Story

In the late nineties (yep, even before Y2K!), I was the first to launch telework for a federal government agency in Southern California. While the bureaucracy in DC had some written policy, this was new turf and there was little more than vague direction and forms (surprise, governmental forms!). I knew this would be a challenge since there were so many decisions to be made and questions to be answered. Who should work at home? How would I lead those I could not see throughout the day? Could I even muster up the trust to feel comfortable that people working from their homes were actually working? These and many more questions flooded my mind so much so that I thought I was developing a twitch! Nonetheless, I took a deep breath and began this new leadership journey.

At first, I concentrated on the logistical elements. I ordered new computers, had the necessary software installed (keep in mind not everything was *plug and play* back then, and remote software updates did not yet exist). So I set about creating internal processes for home-based employees and I created a budget to support them. Then I physically closed down the old brick and mortar office. I honestly believed my work was done! NOT!!!

The real work of encouraging, motivating, training, inspiring, and positively influencing my virtual employees still needed major honing on my part. I recall as I worked through these mandates, there were new dilemmas of dealing with the unique challenges that each employee was facing. One of these employees was Chris, an information technology manager. I recall when I periodically touched base with Chris, the spark in his voice was beginning to wane. One day, about three months in to the telework project I confronted the issue straight-on. Chris told me that while he really enjoyed the autonomy of working at home, he would hear his internal voice beckoning him to the kitchen refrigerator! In a mere three months, Chris had gained nearly 30 pounds! He was beside himself for his lack of discipline.

Chris went on to say that when he was the proverbial office worker, he had many years of well-defined habits that disappeared seemingly overnight! He no longer "suited up" for work in the morning. He no longer stopped at Starbuck's for his morning coffee on his way to the office. He no longer got into the office and chatted with his coworkers, nor did he have a predefined lunchtime to hang out with his cronies! For Chris, working at home brought unfettered access to a well-stocked kitchen. He began his day wearing slippers and eating a large breakfast of bacon, eggs, and a Danish! For Chris, doing his job at home brought him the new found freedom of snacking throughout the day!

As Chris told me his tale of woe, I felt profoundly responsible for his new unhealthy habits. I felt I was truly missing the mark on the people side of the organizational equation. At this point I realized that putting people to work in the virtual space was more than logistics and administrivia! So Chris and I began brainstorming (it's important to ensure people are part of the people-process) new healthy habits to replace the unhealthy ones. Jointly, Chris and I decided that when he and I spoke each day he would walk outside. Fortunately, the Southern California weather is quite cooperative for this sort of thing! We also decided that it would be helpful for him to meet with his clients more. And finally we decided that he would replace the unhealthy food in his kitchen with healthier alternatives. As a result, Chris was able to lose most of the extra "baggage" he had gained.

The Theory

In an age of re-engineering, re-purposing, and re-tooling; perhaps nothing is as pervasive as re-defining the art of work. That's right, basic everyday work. The kind of work we do to support our families, pay the mortgage, and put food on the table. How is it possible that what used to be a highly supervised, single location, 9 to 5 workday has morphed into an incredibly flexible environment where work is performed in a house, a car, a conference room, and yes—even on the beach? And where is the leader, manager, or supervisor in this world? That's right, invisible!

It is almost impossible to believe that the concept of working virtually had its beginnings some 42 years ago. The history of virtual work, or as some call it telework, began in 1972, when Jack Nilles, "The Father of Telecommuting", then a University of Southern California researcher, merged the idea of telecommunication with transportation. In 1981 J.C. Penney launched its first call center of home-based catalogue order-takers. Eventually the federal government took note and offered its first official endorsement of telecommuting in 1993.[1]

Unfortunately, the early years of telecommuting were best characterized in terms of technology and policy—and the leadership needs of the virtual worker were ignored. Organizations only sought to ensure virtual workers had the hardware and software to do their work and that the policy and paperwork were created to document the procedures of working from home. The fact is that working as a virtual employee can be extremely isolating. It can be being perceived as "out of sight, out of mind". It can mean being forgotten when it comes to training opportunities. It can mean little possibility for promotion. In fact, it can be a downright sad and depressing experience. By 2000, organizations realized something was missing—it was the people and cultural side of the equation!

As a result, the onslaught of virtual work brought with it a number of critical people areas that needed to be addressed prior to launching virtual organizations. These areas include the social, political, economic, legal, intercultural, and technological aspects of invisible leadership.[2] Your role as an effective invisible leader is to address your leadership style in the context of these elements. To support you in the invisible leadership journey, this book examines a new leadership model to help you create a productive organization that allows you to meet your numbers and sleep better. Implementing this leadership model will ensure your virtual employees feel valued, important, and trusted. As a result, you will pave the way to the consummately successful virtual organization.

The Takeaway

Virtual organizations are here to stay. The stats tell us the following.

- 40% more U.S. employers offer flexible workplace options than they did five years ago.

- Regular telecommuting grew 115% in the past decade, nearly 10 times faster than the rest of the workforce.

- The entire work-at-home population is 10 to 15 times larger than full-time employees who work at home half-time or more.[3]

Your role as an invisible leader is probably more complicated and labor intensive than you believed when you "signed up" for the task! To succeed, you will need to negotiate the people side of the invisible leadership equation. You will need to support the social side of your remote employees. You will need to trust your invisible employees. You will need to defend your team more than ever on the political front. You will need to invest to keep your invisible team trained. You will need to keep them in mind for promotions. You will need to remain aware of the legal ramifications of leading people who do not come to the office. You will need a greater understanding about the cultural nuances of a dispersed team. And you will need to ensure that your team is kept up to speed technologically so they don't turn into digital dust! At the end of the day meeting your numbers and getting the sleep you deserve comes down to your effectiveness as an invisible leader where your invisible employees feel valued, important, and trusted.

Part I

THE INVISIBLE LEADER
IN YOU

*"There are two ways of exerting one's strength;
one is pushing down, the other is pulling up."*

—Booker T. Washington

Chapter 1

THE SUCCESSFUL INVISIBLE ORGANIZATION DEFINED

"The concept of the 'virtual organization' is essential to understanding how new business works."

—*Tom Peters*

Before we can move into the "How To's" of invisible leadership take a look at the "as is" side of your organization. After all, how will you know if your virtual organization is successful if you don't know the metrics for your brick and mortar organization? There's really not much point in tossing and turning over the numbers, if you don't know what you should be measuring! Finding out how far you have come means first knowing where you were. Research has shown that there are five factors that drive a successful virtual organization. These five factors include employee productivity [4], employee retention [5], employee attendance [6], professional development of employees [7], and promotions of employees.[8] Hence the success of the virtual organization is measured by evaluating the before and after numbers of these five elements.

The Story

Having worked in the federal space for quite some time, tracking metrics and responding to data calls was a way of life. So when the time came to transition my team to an invisible workforce I was well-equipped with my pre-transition numbers. I had maintained data on everything from client satisfaction to revenue, training, attrition, promotions, as well as bonuses and recognition. As we moved through transition I noted that I started to receive suggestions for additional training. I also received mounting requests for promotions. Unfortunately, given the bureaucratic structure of the organization coupled with the belief in HQ that virtual workers already "had it made", my requests for additional funding met with such resistance that it ultimately led to falling performance numbers. Something had to change. So I learned early on that effectively leading a virtual workforce required more leadership than ever before. It meant "going to bat" more frequently for my invisible employees. It meant being more available to listen to their opinions and suggestions. And it meant caring enough to be consistently mindful of how unnoticed, isolated, and untrained my team could become in the future. These actions on my part coupled with initiating a peer reward system went a long way to retain and make this team become even more successful than they were in the past.

The Theory

While productivity, retention, attendance, training, and promotions define success in a successful virtual organization, the primary driver behind each of the elements is leadership that has a direct and causal influence on each and every element. Let's consider each of these.

Productivity. In general, one of the benefits of leadership that espouses cohesion and commitment in the virtual environment is increased productivity.[9] In a survey of 83 companies, research found virtual organizations showed improved productivity, lower costs, and a larger talent pool than their brick and mortar counterparts.[10] In addition, a survey of 354 British telecommunications employees data was gathered concerning pre and post telework implementations.[11] All told, the participants found telework to be a positive experience and the post survey of the research indicated that overall productivity improved.

Similarly, in a survey of 563 firms where 37% of the workforce is comprised of full time teleworkers, improvements in productivity were found among the virtual workers.[12] And finally, in a study of six firms conducted in the Netherlands where the prevalence of telework is comparable to the U.S., the results pointed to improved productivity in virtual work environments.[13] In fact, more than two thirds of employers report increased productivity among their teleworkers.[14]

For the most part, increased productivity in the virtual organization requires significant reliance on leadership to ensure employees remain engaged. In terms of specifics, a shift to a virtual workplace involves a thorough change management plan for all parts of the organization. It includes; a gap analysis of people and their stages of professional development, a review of processes, procedures, and policies, and an analysis of safety parameters and security/risk mitigation. Change management should occur in stages using lessons learned and best practices from each phase to improve implementation of subsequent phases. Led well, the journey to a virtual organization can result in productivity gains of 10-40%.[15]

Retention. The cost to replace an employ can take a significant toll on a virtual organization especially when information is not communicated with the remaining members of the team. Replacement costs can be staggering considering advertising, interviewing, recruitment fees, and reference checking. Hence, creating an invisible organization where employees feel valued, important, trusted, and want to stay is crucial.

Research indicates that invisible leaders who recognize, promote, train, render clear expectations, provide engaging assignments and autonomy, enhance the well-being of the invisible employee and increase the odds of retaining the employee.[16] Companies such as AT&T and P&G have launched highly successful virtual organizations on a globalized basis and have found positive benefits in employee retention.[17] The net result is that leaders who remain mindful of the important role virtual workers play in their organization with satisfying assignments and appropriate rewards and recognition are more likely to retain these employees.[18]

Attendance. In general, attendance in the virtual workspace tends to be greater. On a day when employees may be a little tired and prone to call in sick, they tend to take stock of how little effort it takes to get to work. With the reduced stress of no commute, invisible employees are more likely to show up![19] In a virtual organization, the need for team members to be available is important so that projects can move forward. Fortunately, research indicates that the number of hours virtual employees work tends to be greater compared with those in an office setting.[20] The reasons for working more and longer days are varied. Perhaps some may work more to protect the "perk" of telework; others may work more as an attempt to gain greater visibility in an otherwise invisible environment.

Professional development. There is no doubt that development of invisible employees can make for a successful virtual organization. In fact, not only do growth and development provide for ongoing success of the organization by improving performance, they also mitigate the feeling of isolation that can so often be pervasive in the virtual workplace.[21]

It is interesting to note that learning and professional development not only accrue from formal developmental programs, they can also be anchored into the communities of practice that exist in a virtual organization. Communities of practice permit those who are not as well versed in a given discipline, to interact with those who are experienced in that functional area. What is particularly beneficial, in addition to the obvious element of increased knowledge for work performance, is that these communities provided a springboard to enhanced trusting team relationships and team motivation.[22] In sum, the net result is that professional development, in any form, creates a more agile team capable of enhanced collaboration.

Promotions. Leaders sometimes overlook the potential for upward mobility for virtual employees in an organization, as they are more influenced by employees who are physically present.[23] Nonetheless, experts advise leaders of virtual employees to avoid what is known as "management by observation" and they advise leaders to focus on the what and how of the work as opposed to the where and when of the work. Instead of looking for who arrives early and stays late, keep an eye on what has actually been accomplished. Let's face it, in typical office venues, many times promotions were a result of office politics and outright favoritism. With a focus on results, the entire organization, sans the "favorite sons", are happier!

Instead of creating a new performance appraisal system for the virtual organization, the organization as a whole must adopt a new evaluation system that covers all employees, virtual or not. The net result of consistent performance-based promotions is that both the brick and mortar offices, and the virtual offices are more successful.[24]

The Takeaway

In summary, using the same leadership methods as office-based groups, maintaining an out-of-sight out-of-mind mentality, and relegating virtual workers to the level of robotic contributors can cause disengagement of your virtual workers. It can also result in a tendency of virtual workers to delay the workflow, and a loss of well-being that comes from being ignored by leadership. Research tells us that the invisible leader must balance attention to virtual workers while clearly articulating expectations and task assignments. As you build invisible teams, you create social capital where each individual is valued as a contributing member of the team. Simply put, "Leadership makes telework work."[25]

Chapter 2

LEADING IN THE VIRTUAL WORKSPACE: WHERE IS THE INSTRUCTION MANUAL?

"If you are a leader, you should never forget that everyone needs encouragement. And everyone who receives it— young or old, successful or less-than-successful, unknown or famous—is changed by it."

—*John C. Maxwell*

OK—so now that we have a grip on what makes a successful virtual organization and we have gotten an insight on the importance of the special kind of leadership that's required, let's start to focus on you, the invisible leader. As you can probably tell, I like to begin chapters with a story. The next one is very personal to me and makes me feel great every time I think about it. So here goes!

The Story

Encouragement means the world to me; just a few positive words and I am off to the races! I'm sure many of us can recall a special teacher or manager who was able to inspire us to be better students or employees. For me, that inspiration came from my first best-invisible-boss-ever, Carl. Carl worked in downtown San Francisco and I worked in San Diego. Nonetheless, just a quick phone call from Carl at 4 pm provided me with enough encouragement, enthusiasm, motivation, and inspiration to work well into the evening. Carl was the kind of invisible leader who cared deeply about people. He trusted his employees implicitly. He cared about his invisible employees professionally and personally; and he made it a point to check-in with me frequently. While Carl was not a micro manager, in fact he was far from it, he would call and offer encouragement, ask if there was anything he could do to support me in managing my organization, and brainstorm with me ways to help our clients. The operative word here is—brainstorm. Rarely, if ever, did Carl tell me what to do. Instead, *we* routinely brainstormed solutions to our mutual business challenges.

Back in the mid-eighties it was my job to provide IT support to other federal agencies in Southern California. In doing so, I knew I could call upon Carl for advice to take my work to a higher level and find new ways to impress my clients. Carl would often call to run ideas by me and ask my advice about how I could help improve on the ideas. Together, we would spend hours working plans to give clients a better experience with our organization. You'll notice I said **our** clients. I use this word purposefully because Carl always considered us a team. He never used words such as "my idea", "my organization", or (the absolute worst) "my people!" In my opinion, Carl was an incredibly inspiring invisible leader.

But Carl's leadership didn't stop with inspiration and motivation. Carl was also a positive influence, a role model, and the consummate team player on the political front. In a very short time, I came to realize that I was beginning to emulate Carl in my own leadership practices. I would connect with my team with greater frequency and on a level that was more considerate and encouraging. I would take time to honor my team with recognition, praise, and awards as often as possible. As a result, the southern team garnered the highest customer satisfaction scores in the region and routinely exceeded our growth and productivity numbers.

Carl also appreciated the concept of employee development and promotion. Being out of the line of vision of a leader can easily make a virtual employee a forgotten soul when it comes to training and development. Carl never forgot that even though I was more than 500 miles away, I was an integral part of his team and deserved the same opportunities for training as those who were co-located with him. Even when promotions came up, Carl thought of me! During the years I worked for Carl, I received two highly sought after promotions.

But perhaps most important to me, Carl was considerate, understanding, and was always concerned about my welfare. I can recall when I was going through a divorce. Carl would call me daily to see how I was faring and to reassure me that I was a strong person who could get through it. At one point, he even offered up his attorney! Simply put, Carl cared, and as a result I felt confident knowing he would be there to lift me up whenever I needed it. Though Carl had numerous other employees, he always made me feel special and in many ways I believed that Carl saw his life's purpose as helping others succeed and feel special!

It was a sad day for me when Carl retired. I flew to San Francisco and participated in his retirement and cried when I spoke during the ceremony. To this day, many years later, I still think of him frequently. Carl was able to do from afar, what many leaders could not do in person; make a self-perceived insecure young woman realize that she could become better every day!

As you will recall, I began this part of the book with the Booker Washington quote, "*There are two ways of exerting one's strength; one is pushing down, the other is pulling up.*" Thank you Carl, for pulling me up!

The Theory

As we study leadership, we become keenly aware of the myriad of leadership styles that exist. However, due to its unusual nature, the virtual workspace requires something special by way of leadership. So, where is the instruction manual? It's here, in this book!

Let's start the quest for the "how to" by considering that for most teleworkers, the foray into working virtually begins with sheer euphoria! However, for the invisible leader transitioning an individual or even an entire organization into the virtual workspace can present mixed emotions. In the world of virtual organizations we tend to see three widely different leadership camps: the camp that lacks trust in employees and attempts to micro manage every move of the teleworker; the camp that is relieved to have one or more employees "out of sight and out of mind"; and the camp that practices transformational leadership that truly trusts and cares about each virtual employee. Your initial quest for creating your invisible leadership paradigm is to ask yourself (now be honest!), ". . . in which camp do I feel most comfortable?".

The "I don't trust you" leader. In the first camp, the virtual leader distrusts employees working off-site. This is, by far, the most challenging to deal with since this leader will continuously doubt the teleworker is actually working. I have heard of these leaders demanding that virtual employees maintain an "always on" camera on their computers. How unfortunate that these leaders have nothing better to do than observe every move of their virtual employees and micromanage their actions! Even more unfortunate is the plight of those employees who must be careful not to pick their noses or eat Twinkies in front of the computer camera!

Fundamentally, these leaders don't trust their employees to work effectively while at home. They believe these employees will spend considerable time watching TV, surfing the web, working out, taking care of kids, and the list goes on and on. For leaders with this belief system a strong invisible leadership development program with an emphasis on trust should be mandatory.

The "leave me alone" leader. In the second leadership camp we have the invisible leader who is relieved to have employees out of the office. The first words out of this leader's mouth are

". . . whew—thank goodness they're gone . . .!" In this camp we
see a situation where the virtual employee is ignored, is not given
ongoing training, and is rarely considered for promotion. All too
often, this virtual leader begins to devalue the virtual employee
from the moment the employee relocates to the invisible venue.
Most often this leader only makes contact via email with some
form of demand for a deliverable or to put an employee on notice
that he or she has made a mistake. In this scenario, the employee
is "pushed down" by not being acknowledged and only recognized for errors and problems.

Ensuring your virtual employees feel valued is an essential
component for the invisible employee to perform well. Employees who are shown they are valuable to the organization by direct
statements and by responsiveness on your part can begin and
end their work day on a positive note and provide better work
products.

The "pull people up" leader. It is blatantly unfair and non-pro-
ductive to lead in ways described above. It is only the very
savvy leader who understands the personal/people angle needed
in the virtual space. In this third camp we find invisible leaders who recognize that leading virtually actually requires more
leadership, not less—it requires Transformational Leadership.
It means leading with consideration and understanding that the
virtual employee is out there alone. It means leading to inspire
and motivate. It means ensuring the job is intellectually stimulating. And it means reflecting a model of leadership behavior
that employees want to emulate. Overall, this leadership "pulls

people up", encourages growth, and offers a positive career path ahead.

The Takeaway

Leading in the virtual workspace requires a leadership style that is uplifting. In the most straightforward words, it requires that the invisible leader participates in a developmental program to:

- Have a sense of care and concern for invisible employees
- Be willing to provide appropriate assignments, training, and development
- Actively provide inspiration and motivation through encouragement
- Become a role model of positive influence through trust and empathy.

Chapter 3

LEADERSHIP MAKES TELEWORK, WORK! LOOK BEFORE YOU LEAP

"Look before you leap for as you sow, ye are like to reap."
—*Samuel Butler*

At this point, you may be asking yourself if you are likely to be a successful invisible leader. The human side of the distance equation is even more worthy of examination before you leap into the virtual work paradigm. Using the Invisible Leadership Model, aligned with an associated assessment, you can determine the likelihood of your success as an invisible leader.

The Story

Let's begin this chapter with the story of Martin. Martin worked for me a number of years ago and was an incredible employee. He was the consummate team player and never hesitated to help a colleague. His interpersonal skills were top notch, and his coworkers enjoyed his positive attitude and terrific sense of humor.

Martin's foray into virtual work was quite interesting. When I first floated the idea of Martin working from home, he was delighted! He was so excited I thought I'd have to pull him down from the ceiling! All he could talk about was the independence and autonomy he would have to do his work without the interruptions in the office. Martin thanked me profusely for trusting him to work on his own in this heretofore unconventional way. Given Martin's reaction, you would have thought he just won the lottery!

In what seemed like no time at all (literally three days), Martin started to appear in the office usually at about 2 pm each day. After a few weeks, I approached Martin and asked him "why?". After all of his excitement about being given the "privilege" to work at home, he was still coming into the office each day. With head hung low, Martin proceeded to tell me the only conversation he was having during his work time at home was with his dog who would rather nap that engage in dialogue! Martin then asked if he could come back to the office on a full time basis and be with his colleagues. Of course, I said yes!

There's an old adage that advises us to "look before you leap." It tells us to look at the path ahead and consider challenges along the way. It allows us to evaluate our personal abilities and predilections before we commit to the journey. In his book *Good to Great*, Collins tells us to get the right people on the right bus in the right seats. Such sage advice is critical in the arena of virtual work. Even if the employee is *the right person* and the job is *the right bus*, if working virtually is not *the right seat*, everyone suffers—the employee, the leader, and the organization! As a virtual leader, it is your job to ensure that working virtually is right for the employee.

The Theory

The transition to leading in a virtual environment can be brutally difficult. Leading at a distance is not easy and certainly not everyone is "wired" for the task. Looking for aptitude to lead virtually, requires examining the prospective or current virtual leader from a number of angles and asking the right questions. Consider first the social perspective. This is the most overlooked side of the invisible leadership equation! In fact, as counterintuitive as it may seem, leading virtually has a huge social component. After all, unless you are herding cats or shepherding other animals, leadership involves people! What makes invisible leadership so challenging is that the leader must make the <u>extra</u> effort to reach out to virtual employees.

Goleman tells us that leaders, in general, must relate to their employees in a socially intelligent manner. A manner that provides effectiveness in relationships through empathy.[26] In addition, leaders must also overcome doubts, and trust that their employees are really working and not attending to duties and obligations on the home front. Hence, invisible leadership must address these challenges and develop and use different leadership behaviors to manage at a distance. For example, consistent one-on-one communication with virtual employees that exceeds in-office communication may serve as a tool for creating, enhancing, and maintaining a level of trust. Such communication would serve to mitigate doubts about the virtual employee and send messages that speak to a sense of commitment rather than control. Additionally, well-articulated job metrics can serve to establish appropriate expectations on the part of the leader as well as the virtual worker.[27] After all, without a map and timeline, it's quite impossible for the invisible employee to know your vision and the results you expect.

The Takeaway

The fact is that not everyone is suited to invisible work. As invisible leaders, it is important to understand that one size does not fit all when it comes to a telework paradigm. Take the time to perform a formal self-assessment before doing all of the work associated with creating a virtual organization. And just in case you are already leading in the virtual workspace, you would be wise to assess your competencies and predilection for leading invisibly. In the interim, be sure to check-in with your virtual employees frequently, at least several times a week to make sure they are comfortable in the virtual workspace.

Chapter 4

WHEN IT COMES TO LEADING, WHAT'S YOUR PERSONAL LEADERSHIP STYLE?

"Employees who believe that management is concerned about them as a whole person—not just an employee—are more productive, more satisfied, more fulfilled. Satisfied employees mean satisfied customers, which leads to profitability."
—*Anne Mulcahy, CEO of Xerox*

There are many styles of leadership. Most of us use several leadership styles at one time or another depending on the state of affairs in our organization. Given the nature of the invisible organization, this is a good time to evaluate your leadership style and reflect upon it.

The Story

This is the story about Sam. Sam was a leader who trusted none of his employees; neither those who worked with him in the office, nor those who worked from home. Unfortunately, he trusted those working from home even less than those he could see!

Sam routinely belittled his invisible employees on conference calls; embarrassing them in front of other members of his team. He constantly second-guessed decisions of his virtual employees. And more often than not, Sam would fly off the handle anytime a subordinate offered an opinion different from Sam's (what a way to kill any possibility of creative and innovative thinking!). Sam also had the unnerving habit of calling his teleworkers just before quitting time to check to see if they were still working.

Unfortunately, Sam worked for a corporation that only cared about the revenue, profit, and margins. Sam was never assessed for his capabilities or predilection towards virtual leadership and never participated in a virtual leadership development program. Over the years, Sam saw a constant turnover among his invisible employees; not one of whom even said good-bye to him. Eventually, corporate saw the expensive trend of re-staffing Sam's positions and told him he would need to resign, retire, or be fired. He retired!

The Theory

It is not uncommon to witness controlling leadership behaviors and oftentimes it is grounded in the lack of trust. Let's take a look at three unique leadership styles. These are styles that occur most often in the context of invisible leadership and each of them carries with it a different degree of trust in remote employees. Researchers cite the following three models that define the relationship between a leader and follower in the virtual environment.[28]

Transactional leadership. The first leadership style to consider is what is known as the transactional or governance relationship theory between a leader and a follower. It lends itself to control and can cause distrust. This approach is consistent with the notion that, in general, managers do not want to relinquish control or power and tend to exhibit little, if any, trust in their employees.[29] This type of leadership can lead to a hostile work environment especially when disciplinary threats loom large. It is, in fact, described as a leadership paradigm that is both counterproductive and ineffective. In the virtual sphere the untrusting transactional leader can be the "kiss of death" for themselves, the employees, and the organization. Leaders who fall into this category should be assessed and developed to lead in a manner that is trusting and supportive of virtual employees.

Contingency/situational leadership. The second leadership model, contingency leadership theory (sometimes referred to as situational leadership), speaks to an exchange relationship where responsibilities and expectations adjust to the work at hand. Though contingency leadership can have an intuitive appeal since it prescribes adapting style to situation, it tends to be grounded in lack of trust on the parts of the leader as well as the virtual employees. Contingency leadership tends to focus on outcomes vice processes since there are unique situations and requirements in play at any given time. This tends to cause uncertainty on the part of the employees who wonder what will be important today!

Transformational leadership. A look at transformational leadership starts with a look at the work of Bennis who states,

". . . leaders are people who do the right thing; managers are people who do things right".[30] In this context, the transformational leader understands the importance of vision, goals, empowerment, and trust. Each of these elements ties closely with Bennis' leadership themes of employee significance, team spirit, excitement, motivation, and quality outcomes. Traits such as these make the odds of success for the invisible leader greater. Making the adjustment to leading a virtual organization is not intuitive[31], and while it requires attention to administrative details such as equipment and software, it also means leading employees in a more mindful manner with a consistent vigilance focused on the needs and feelings of the remote employee.

In this style, leader and follower work together as partners with the leader fostering involvement and inclusion and an end goal of seeing a fully engaged employee with even better performance.[32] While acting as a transformational leader, the leader must also give consideration to affinity, operational, and temporal differences. This means addressing the geographical separation from the virtual workers, differences in operational nuances from one virtual worker to another, and physical differences such as multiple time zones.[33]

Whereas transactional leadership tends to be task oriented and contingency leadership is outcome oriented, transformational leadership is employee oriented. This third construct is the cooperative approach to leadership where trust is the cornerstone of the working relationship. This style is most closely aligned with a successful virtual workforce.[34]

The Takeaway

The takeaway for this chapter reads like the story of the Three Little Pigs. Much like invisible leadership styles taking on the challenge of building a virtual organization, the three pigs each had a different strategy for dealing with their task. One built his house easily out of straw being proud that he knew-it-all when it came to dealing with threats. The second built his house out of wood going for the good looks and reasonably priced supplies. The last little pig put his whole heart into his house of bricks. It was a lot more work, but he knew if he stuck to it he would be successfully protected.

So too, for virtual leaders. An invisible leader can act tough and be a know-it-all, but that eventually falls apart when employees see this approach as offensive, and start jumping ship. Alternatively, an invisible leader can change course with each project and ignore the fact that there are real people on the other side of the holographic wall. Real people need consistent consideration, motivation, intellectual stimulation, and an authentic leader. And it is in this vein that real success accrues to the leader who can commit to, trust, develop, acknowledge, and reward virtual employees—this is the consummate invisible leader!

Part II

THE DYNAMICS OF SUCCESSFUL INVISIBLE LEADERSHIP

Chapter 5

THE INVISIBLE SOCIAL DYNAMIC

"I suppose leadership at one time meant muscles; but today it means getting along with people."

—*Mahatma Gandhi*

Relationships become stronger or weaker based on social connectedness and mutual respect. A willingness to communicate and a real and genuine concern for another becomes the fulcrum for a balanced and successful relationship. Without the social bonds, relationships will wither over time.

The Story

At one point in my career I lived in San Francisco and one of my teams was located in San Diego. I recall one of my team members, Ben, who was in the San Diego Office. Ben was incredibly dependable, conscientious, and an all-around great guy. There was no task or project too complex for Ben. And maybe more importantly, I never lost sleep worrying if he would complete it perfectly! Ben and I had a wonderful rapport and I believe it's because we never missed an opportunity to connect. We would have frequent telephone calls, lots of emails, and impromptu chats about more than work. I recall on one visit to San Diego, I met with Ben and told him I was looking at buying a stick-shift car. Before I could ask, I was in his black TransAm getting a refresher lesson in driving a stick-shift! Eventually, I moved back to San Diego and to this day, some 14 years later, Ben and I get together for coffee regularly. For me, there is nothing better than a strong relationship to make an invisible organization hum.

The Theory

Since it is so easy for an individual or a team to become lost and isolated in the virtual organization, keeping an eye on the social aspect of the team is of paramount importance. One of the most critical functions of a leader in a virtual environment is to be a model team player and set the stage, terms, and conditions for his/her team members to successfully be a part of the virtual teamwork environment.[35] Creating something akin to a well-functioning virtual family is an important facet to creating and sustaining a productive and successful invisible team. A leader who is people oriented provides a form of social influence through inspiration. This orientation subsequently yields motivation and commitment on the part of followers, and results in a team that works well independently.[36] From a social vantage point, the invisible leader must become an almost parental influence. This influence, however, needs to be balanced—no helicopter parenting here!

Leadership needs to encourage and empower followers to self-lead.[37] Formal training for invisible leaders should include social cues in an anonymous environment, social protocol, and cultural intelligence. This means that virtual leaders must evolve to new levels of collaboration, socialization, and communication since all three support the leaders' ability to better guide, inspire, and motivate an invisible family. By involving virtual employees and giving them a say in decision making, the invisible leader recognizes family members by acknowledging and respecting the know-how and expertise each member brings to the team.

Much like a geographically dispersed family, where parents need to make a greater effort to connect with family members, the invisible leader needs to make an extra effort to interface with virtual employees more than they do with in-office employees. Without this extra effort a feeling of isolation can develop and negatively affect the virtual employee in terms of feeling ignored, inconsequential, and not providing value and contribution to the organization.[38] Isolation is one of the most daunting situations facing virtual employees where such feelings can lead to lower job satisfaction and increased turnover. It is important for invisible leaders to understand that this challenge exists for all virtual employees but is especially greater for those who live alone or are relatively new to an organization.

When you think about it, one of the worst punishments in the prison system is solitary confinement. The repercussions of isolation have been shown to have far reaching effects both psychologically and physically. It is known to impair the immune function and boost inflammation, and can lead to arthritis, type-2 diabetes, and heart disease. Loneliness breaks our hearts, literally.[39] On emotional and psychological levels, isolation keeps us from exchanging energy with others which can result in fuzzy

thinking and even depression. Therefore, it is extremely important for the virtual leader to check-in with employees frequently,
socialize the team, engage employees to share personal information, and create mentor-protégé arrangements of collaboration.[40]

An additional way to engender the social element in the invisible organization is to recognize individuals who work virtually
since it is easy for their contributions to go unnoticed. Since virtual employees do not have the luxury of receiving kudos while
visiting the office coffee machine with their leaders, invisible
leaders need to remind themselves to offer congratulatory com-
ments and gratitude for a job well done through phone calls as
well as personal communications and messages.[41]

The Takeaway

All told, there is a need for invisible leaders to focus on the
social element in the virtual organization. They need to make
a concerted effort and a significant investment in knowing and
understanding each virtual employee. And they need to develop
and maintain a one-to-one relationship that focuses on each
employee's professional and personal dreams and goals.[42]

Virtual organizations are becoming increasingly common.
While these organizations can be extremely productive several
challenges exist. Among them is communication that requires
more effort, more frequency, and more conciseness. There are
also feelings of isolation, and a lack of social interface and rapport.
As an invisible leader, you must communicate clearly, honestly,
frequently, and promptly. It is also your task to build and sustain
relationships. If you are located in the same city as your invisible

employees, occasionally plan lunch or happy hour together—or even plan a walking meeting! If distance does not permit this, connect via social media. Bottom line is to demonstrate in tangible ways that you genuinely value your invisible employees.

Chapter 6

THE POLITICAL HEADWINDS

"Sometimes doing a good job at work is like wetting your pants in a dark suit—you get a warm feeling, but nobody else notices."

—*Author Unknown*

Have you ever felt that trying to get an "atta-boy/atta-girl" required more work than the work itself? Working in a highly political virtual environment can be a daunting experience, especially as people jockey for position. For the great majority it seems to require an all-out full court press of a campaign to bring a spotlight to your work products and organizational successes. For the invisible leader, this means becoming a cheerleader both for yourself and for your virtual employees.

The Story

A while back I worked in a field office and had virtual employees in various locations. Since I did not work at headquarters, I too was considered an invisible employee. This made my staff members even more invisible! As a result, I did everything I could to call attention to important projects my team was supporting.

47

Sharing the spotlight with my invisible employees was critical to getting the perks, attention, and recognition they deserved but due to virtual distance, would not receive.

At one point, my team had done an incredible job creating and launching a nationwide initiative. Given the success of the project, I was invited to come to HQ to receive a very visible and important national award. This became the perfect time to request that the award be shared with all of my invisible employees who had actually done the vast majority of the heavy lifting of the project. As a result of the notoriety that otherwise might not have occurred, many of these employees became part of succession planning and received promotions. The bottom line is that virtual work can frequently go unnoticed with the up-line unless a virtual leader makes the effort to put a spotlight on invisible employees and the invisible organization as a whole.

The Theory

The political side of the invisible organization is difficult to navigate. Most times, as an invisible leader, you are faced with expending rigorous effort simply to make your organization and your virtual employees get noticed for all that is accomplished. Unfortunately, this requires that you go the extra mile to market your team. There are various vectors that influence political success for those who reside in an invisible organizational bubble; these include empowerment, recognition, and promotion. Retaining virtual employees can be daunting when they feel they are forgotten souls who may never receive a plum assignment or a place in the corporate succession plan.

The fact is that every organization faces politics. Whether the forces of politics are localized, national, or global, leaders must be constantly aware of the potential force of such headwinds. This is especially so for the invisible leader. Simply developing the case for a telework environment with the powers-that-be can involve considerable effort. This is especially true when one's up line is not supportive of the idea at the start. In this situation you, as the invisible leader, can expect that your numbers concerning productivity and revenue will be watched closely by those above you in the organization. Initially, you may receive kudos for reducing the overhead expenses associated with office space, but ultimately, you will need to prove your organization is at least as productive as it was in the pre-telework days. One of the best ways to spur on productivity is through empowerment.

The politics of empowerment. Empowerment allows "one who leads others to lead themselves"[43] and create an organization of responsibility, initiative, and confidence. While some leaders believe sharing power means sharing political power and possibly loosing footing within the corporation, empowerment really means giving invisible employees the latitude to make decisions regarding their own work. Hence, desired empowerment on the part of the virtual worker underscores autonomy in their own work.[44]

The overall intent of empowerment is to ensure that team members see themselves as valued, trusted, and empowered partners.[45] Ultimately, empowerment results in employees who perceive themselves as significant, feel like part of the team family, are excited and passionate about their work, and produce quality outcomes/products.[46] In a virtual workspace, knowledge-based technology environments are more conducive to the empowering methods of transformational leadership.[47] Virtual work environments are just such environments and should involve leadership that deemphasizes supervision and control, and provides for individual and team empowerment.[48] As a result, there is an increase in overall productivity and job satisfaction among employees, as well as a decrease in absenteeism.

The politics of recognition. One of the most often overlooked elements of positive leadership in virtual teams is feedback to individual team members in the form of effective appraisals that highlight the contributions of the invisible employee to the success of the overall team.[49] Most leaders recognize the need to give a pat on the back to employees who are visibly "in their face" as this serves to keep peace on the office home front. Because of this, the virtual employee must actually maneuver to obtain recognition. I have known teleworkers to take it upon themselves to write-up and message their noteworthy accomplishments weekly, just to get a modicum of recognition from an invisible leader. Oftentimes, this is the way an invisible employee jockeys for position in a political, albeit invisible, organization.

The politics of promotions. Since virtual leaders are more influenced by employees who are collocated with them, invisible leaders can tend to overlook the potential for upward mobility for virtual employees. In fact, in a virtual organization, employees may not be in a position to be considered for promotions and special projects. This is particularly true if leadership in the virtual environment does not pay attention to virtual employees on an individual level, and virtual employees come to feel disconnected and isolated.[50]

Overall, unless leadership evaluates individuals on an objective metric-based model, virtual employees can suffer from lower evaluations, fewer promotions, and smaller pay raises. It is unfortunate when leadership evaluates performance subjectively on merits of simply working in the corporate office. This is known as the concept of *passive face time* and can influence a leader's impression of an employee. This impression is formed when an employee is seen in the hallways, coming to work early, or staying late.[51]

Research indicates there are expected face times (during normal work hours) and extracurricular face times (before and after normal work hours); and these face times are noted by both superiors and coworkers. Research shows that for those employees who presented extra face time, managers were 25% more likely to evaluate these employees as dedicated or committed and 9% more likely to be seen as dependable or responsible.[52]

The invisible leader has also been known to overlook a virtual employee when it comes to promotions. Let's face it, promotions are a scarce commodity and when it comes time to dole them out they usually go to those employees who are in the line of site. So how does this come to be? It generally begins with the plum projects and assignments being given to those employees who are in the locus of power. When a promotion becomes available, the only logical person to be promoted is the one who is in the office and has been groomed and positioned for success. Therefore, it is incumbent on invisible leaders to ensure regular communication with virtual employees, such that they receive assignments of notoriety; that their performance metrics are articulated; and that they are recognized for promotions as appropriate.

The Takeaway

Whether it's *Big P Politics* or *little p politics* it is so easy for the invisible employee to become politically disconnected from both the immediate organization and the HQ. As an invisible leader, you are the only person who can insure that your invisible employees have the political lifelines necessary to recognize the political winds that may be changing and impacting them. You are also the only conduit for recognition and promotions for your invisible employees. In order for your organization to be successful, it is critical that you keep your team connected to the organization at all levels—otherwise you may not keep them at all!

Specifically, as an invisible leader it is important to:

- keep virtual employees engaged by offering ongoing feedback and ensuring they feel connected to the organization
- include them in succession planning efforts for the organization
- exert a positive influence on the promotions of virtual employees by mentoring and assigning enriching and visible projects.

Chapter 7

ECONOMICS: WHEN IT'S ALL SAID AND DONE, FOLLOW THE MONEY! REALLY?

"Not everything that can be counted counts, and not everything that counts can be counted."

—*Albert Einstein*

Sometimes it's easy to ignore or even miss what matters! We are beset with statements and questions like the following. What are your numbers? Did you meet your numbers this quarter? What are you going to do to improve your numbers? And in the midst and flurry of the business of doing business, we can lose sight of the invisible drivers. We call them human resources and many times forget the fact that they are human; and that they are the resources that keep our businesses afloat!

The Story

I'll never forget the first time I set up a virtual organization. It was a hybrid of two offices; one in San Diego and one in Oakland, California. Obviously, being in San Diego, I was the on-site leader to one office and the invisible leader to the other. However, this arrangement was further complicated by the fact that each of the offices was comprised of on-site and virtual employees. The work centered on the first Information Technology (IT) contract of its kind; a contract that could be used by all federal agencies, eliminating the need for redundant contracting actions across hundreds of contracting shops. This was truly a high risk, high visibility, and grass roots endeavor.

For my organization this meant: doing work that had never been done before; providing a service to people who did not understand or necessarily want it (resistance to change); and leading a staff who didn't know if they were about to embark on a great adventure or a career ender! I recall the revenue at the end of the first month in business; our collective net profit was only $38.00! This problem, however, was an opportunity in disguise; for it gave me the chance to involve each member of my team in the solution. O'Toole and Bennis say, "...leaders need to make a conscious decision to support transparency and create a culture of candor." Our financial discussion was our first chance at real and open two-way communication. The extent of our open communication I had never seen before (and may never again)! The fact is that the $38.00 incident set the stage for the free flow of information and ideas for growth for both the in-office and the virtual employees. This was our collective chance to openly and honestly discuss the tough issues that impacted us at that point and would continue to confront us in the future—the numbers!

Needless to say, I wasn't getting much sleep during the early days of that business venture. My biggest goal was to do everything

I could to help and leverage my blended team to perform the best they could. This meant that even the invisible part of the team receive as much of my attention as the visible part. My research had taught me that there are times in developing a virtual organization that require visibility and this was one of them. During the early days to help achieve this, I traveled frequently to the Bay Area and met with everyone for on-site meetings, lunches and evening dinners.

For everyone, life happens that has nothing to do with work. Time and again, there were life issues that arose for my team members. Being sensitive and concerned about the personal welfare of my team topped my list. As people had challenges with their health, their children, their parents, their work-life balance, etc. these challenges needed my empathetic concern. I recall when my primary contracting officer was dealing with the impending death of her mother. She tried to remain courageous at the office, but she really needed to focus on what was happening within her family. I worked to redesign her work location and schedule, to the extent that she worked only when she really needed a distraction from the challenge she was facing at home. I also made myself available whenever she needed to think out loud. When it came to my team especially the invisible component, I consistently made it a priority to take time to show concern and empathy, and to offer support in any way possible. Oftentimes, this meant just listening!

By the way, only the first month was a $38 month. As time went by, our numbers skyrocketed, our team members flourished, and some even recall it as the best job they ever had! They were the **HUMAN** *resources* that made our organization a success!

The Theory

It seems nothing moves business like old fashioned money! And the move to the virtual workplace offers just that—plenty of money saved year on year. Economics and technology were the primary drivers toward the creation of the virtual workplace; economics acted as the reason and technology as the facilitator of this workplace transformation. Employers save financially by reducing the costs associated with physical footprints, and employees save commute time as well as commute costs. The fact is that economic challenges and technology associated with a global economy have created a platform for a more connected workforce in more disconnected venues.

In fact, the market, prices, and globalization are the tipping points that have driven changes in how businesses have evolved and now operate in a virtual setting.[53] Employing a virtual workforce offers a leveraged financial position as it provides for reduced leased office space, permits greater flexibility for scheduling customer support, supports geographically dispersed teams, and offers an advantage in acquiring niche talent and expertise.[54]

Overall, across government and industry, the virtual workforce is expected to continue to increase.[55] In fact, approximately 80% of employees tend to favor working virtually, and more than a third of Americans indicate they would opt for working virtually rather than receive an increase in pay![56] From the employees' vantage point, the positives include the savings of commute time to the office; which amounts to as much as eight work weeks per year in an average roundtrip 40 minute commute.[57] Employees also cite the financial savings in terms of transportation, as well as the ability to react quickly to emergencies on the home front.[58]

In addition to advantages for employees, employers have also fared well. In 2011, surveys from 83 companies in the United States and Canada reported their primary reason for migrating to virtual teams was financially driven. In fact, the companies reported as much as a 21% savings by moving to a virtual workforce model.[59] In addition, as employers continued to migrate their employees to a virtual setting, many organizations reported increases in productivity in the range of 10-20%; with some reporting as much as a 40% increase in productivity.[60]

All told, there are tremendous economic benefits associated with a successful virtual workforce. Employees are positively predisposed to working virtually and find personal and professional benefits associated with teleworking. Employers experience a reduction in operating costs along with an increase in employee productivity resulting in increased revenue and improved margins.

The economic implications of employee attrition. Maintaining in-house tacit knowledge is valuable and near impossible to access after an employee leaves an organization. All told, there are several economic elements associated with employee attrition including the cost to recruit, loss of corporate memory, and impact to other team members. In fact, it has been documented that the time, effort, and expense associated with losing an employee can be substantial since it includes separation costs, vacancy costs, and acquisition costs. For example, advertising, referral fees, recruiting fees, preparing and conducting interviews, and reference checking can comprise a significant portion of the overall expense of employee replacement. In addition to hiring, training costs, as well as decreased productivity further compound the economic challenge of losing talent. Overall, in professional and knowledge-based industries the costs associated with replacing a lost employee can be more than the annual salary of the employee.[61] It is up to strong invisible leaders to make their virtual employees feel valued, important, and trusted since this is what it takes to keep employees.[62]

Over time, companies such as AT&T, IBM, and P&G have launched highly successful virtual organizations on a globalized basis and have found positive benefits in employee retention, loyalty, collaboration, and job satisfaction.[63] The net result is that invisible leaders who remain mindful of the important role virtual workers play in their organization with satisfying assignments and appropriate rewards and recognition are more likely to retain these employees.[64]

The economic implications of improved attendance. Compared to their counterparts who work in a brick and mortar venue, virtual workers tend to experience less stress, less burnout, and less emotional exhaustion than employees who work in the traditional office environments.[65] Little or no commute and a quiet environment that lends itself to enhanced concentration contribute to a greater sense of well-being and reduced absenteeism for the invisible employee.[66] Further, virtual workers experience higher job satisfaction than their in-office counterparts, again resulting in lower rates of absenteeism.[67]

The Takeaway

The economic reality of successfully leading a virtual organization is impressive. The latest telecommuting trend data of Global Workplace Analytics July, 2018 states, if those with compatible jobs and a desire to work from home did so just half the time (roughly the national average for those who do so regularly) the national savings would total over $700 Billion! The report highlights the major contributing factors which include:

- Typical businesses would save $11,000 per person per year

- Telecommuters would save between $2,000 and $7,000 a year

- The greenhouse gas reduction would be equal to taking the entire New York State workforce permanently off the road

- The Congressional Budget Office's estimate of the entire five-year cost of implementing telework throughout government ($30 million) is less than a third of the cost of lost productivity from a single day shutdown of federal offices in Washington DC due to snow ($100 million).

In sum, the current role of the virtual workforce is largely influenced and driven by "relentless change, ferocious competition, and an unstoppable innovation technological evolution." It is fired by economic need and technological presence that enables workers from different global locations to innovate by sharing ideas and concepts.[68]

Chapter 8

THE LEGAL SIDE OF THE BARGAIN

"Laws are not invented; they grow out of circumstances."

—*Azarias*

Go ahead, ask your legal department anything and you will likely to hear, "it depends" as the answer! Then you will get a list of things *it* depends on—all you really wanted was an easy straightforward answer to your question. Instead, you are facing a laundry list of items you now need to research. Just when you thought you would be able to send people home to work and that you could put your organization on autopilot, things got complicated and you entered the world of *what if*. *What if* someone gets hurt while working from home? *What if* one of your invisible employees trips on an extension cord? *What if* you want to revoke telework? Worse yet, *what if* you want to revoke telework from just one individual? What about possible discrimination suits if you terminate telework for an employee? And the list goes on and on! Making decisions about how, when, and to whom the legal considerations of remote work will apply becomes an integral part of the transition to the virtual workspace.

The Story

When I first implemented a virtual organization, it was for the federal government. Having spent my share of time working for the feds, I certainly encountered bureaucracy, administrivia, and lots of paperwork! In fact, I thought I had seen it all until it was time to put telework into action. It seemed for every question my organization posed, there was another form created that had to be filled out. And my soon-to-be virtual employees had many, many questions. These are some of the more interesting ones. Will the government buy new office furniture for my home? Since I will be using more heat or air conditioning working from home, will I be reimbursed for the added utility expense? Will the government pay for my internet service? And the list seemed to grow longer with every passing day. Obviously, the legal department needed to weigh in on the viability of the requests, again complicating the process and adding to the timeline!

However, the most interesting questions that arose were the ones that concerned performance. Not every employee (virtual or not) is a stellar employee. Such was the case with Lawrence. Lawrence was subpar in terms of the quality and quantity of work he produced. He was also naturally argumentative. Nonetheless, in order to be fair, I offered telework to all of my employees in the Los Angeles Area. Though doubts lingered in the back of my mind to permit Lawrence to work from home I still did it. You know, sometimes you need to pay attention to that voice in your head that shouts, ". . . run, Forrest, run!" Well, working virtually for Lawrence turned out to be a nightmare and I finally had to bring him back on site to work. When I told him, he yelled, screamed, and hollered that he was being discriminated against. Finally, and when all of the flying paperwork finally settled down, and Lawrence was told he legally lost his fight to continue to work from home, Lawrence retired!

The Theory

There are two areas in the legal realm of the virtual workspace—internal corporate policy and external regulations.

Internal policy. This is where organizational policy is defined for telework and includes:

- A definition of the corporate baseline telework policy
- How employees can apply to work off-site
- Who is permitted to work from home and how eligibility is determined
- A definition of success metrics including revenue and productivity statistics, employee retention and attendance, training logs, and promotion actions
- A plan for dealing with and resolving disputes
- Defining mediation and arbitration guidelines
- Resources including software technology, hardware and equipment, security, internet access, phone service, and furniture
- Defining how virtual work can be terminated
- Defining review periods

- Using a beta test as a pilot study to initiate a formal telework program

- Defining timelines for performance, responsiveness, goals, metrics, and benchmarks

- Requiring employees acquire child care arrangements for all times a parent is teleworking

- Stating explicitly that telework is not an entitlement.[69]

It is important to note that for a virtual employee, losing the telework accommodation can be upsetting and disheartening, and can result in a loss of performance or even the loss of the employee. The moral here is to tread lightly and seriously consider the ramifications of initiating and terminating telework.

External regulations. The Occupational Safety and Health Act (OSHA) established the ground rules around safety in the workplace as well as reporting requirements surrounding injuries and illness on the job.[70] In February 2000, OSHA set up distinct policies for home worksites in which administrative work is performed via computer. Major elements in the policies include that OSHA will not inspect this type of worksite, and that employers are not liable for these worksites. Though OSHA still takes complaints from employees, they do not take follow-up actions.[71] While this may be good news for employers, the safety of employees should be addressed in employer policy.

Another legal factor goes to workers' compensation. In general, workers' compensation is payable to employees who work from home. However, the rules and guidelines vary from state to state.[72] Therefore, legal experts within a company will need to be conversant with the state-to-state nuances concerning workers' compensation, encourage safety, and stress the importance of ergonomic furnishings for employees while they work from home.

Finally, the Fair Labor Standards Act (FLSA) and Non-Exempt Employees telework applies to both exempt and non-exempt employees. For non-exempt teleworkers a time tracking system with remote access is required as well as clear policy for defining hours worked, overtime definition, and expectations.

The Takeaway

Mitigating risk and ensuring the safety of invisible employees is important. Start with internal policy and address privacy and confidentiality. Be sure security is addressed as a high priority as is the physical safety of teleworkers. Look at the regulatory side from OSHA, to Workers Comp, to the FLSA, to the implications of ADA. Teleworkers may be invisible employees, but they are still members of your organizational family and valuable resources who are integral to the success of your organization.[73]

Chapter 9

THE INTERCULTURAL ELEMENT

"Until I came to IBM, I probably would have told you that culture was just one among several important elements in any organization's makeup and success—along with vision, strategy, marketing, financials, and the like... I came to see, in my time at IBM, that culture isn't just one aspect of the game, it is the game. In the end, an organization is nothing more than the collective capacity of its people to create value."
—*Louis Gerstner, Former CEO of IBM*

Years ago, with the exception of a small number of contractor support staff, and in the days before mass outsourcing, the work environment was easily defined as a group of people who worked in the same place within the same culture, during the same hours, performing the same face-to-face job function.[74] Bookkeepers worked in offices with other bookkeepers from *9 to 5*; typists worked in a typing pool with other typists, etc. The work culture and workforce were well defined and leaders knew exactly where their employees were and what their employees were doing at any given time (breaks included).

Today, your leadership in the work environment is blended since it includes both in-office and virtual work settings as well as employees from differing cultures. As such, the topic of cultural intelligence has become popular and means that you, as a leader in the virtual workspace, must become increasingly aware of cultural nuances and how to navigate in the best way possible to ensure optimal performance across a wide swath of culturally diverse invisible employees.

The Story

Let me tell you about Tina. Tina was a virtual employee of mine and of the Filipino culture. Having done a little research into her culture, I came to understand that the concept of saving face is very important and routed in that culture.[75] Because of this, there is a good news/bad news story.

The good news is that the value of saving face brought the best out in Tina as she was very hardworking. Tina routinely worked late into the evening as evidenced by her late night communications. She worked hard to try to insure her written work products were beyond reproach.

The bad news is that her concept of saving face meant that in order to hide any mistakes she made resulted in interesting stories and denials. At one point in time, I received a complaint from one of Tina's clients who was upset that Tina and a contractor were, as he put it, ". . . having a pissing contest . . . " and he was getting wet! I followed up with a call to Tina to discuss the situation whereupon Tina denied everything the client had shared with me. If this was the first instance of this sort with Tina, I would have ruled it a "he said, she said" situation. But I had experienced this kind of situation many times before with Tina and I came to know that denial was Tina's way of saving face.

Understanding that saving face is so import in Tina's culture, I changed my approach such that I would recharacterize her mistakes with a built-in excuse. This permitted her to look good in spite of the situation. For future encounters, I would begin our conversation with something like, "...I can only imagine how difficult it must be to work as many hours as you do. You must be bleary-eyed and extremely tired by the end of each day. So I am going to ask that you work a shorter day today and then tomorrow take another look at the invoice you sent me. With a good night's rest I'm sure you will be able to make the revisions easily." This time, Tina did not deny the error or blame it on someone else. Instead, since she was able to save face, she reacted in a positive manner. Allowing Tina to save face precluded her being embarrassed and searching for a cover-up.

Respecting cultural values is important in the invisible workspace because it is all too easy to treat everyone the same. For me it was important to keep in mind that treating people fairly did not mean treating everyone identically.

The Theory

We have seen a strong expansion in global enterprises with a compelling vision to attract talent from around the world. Nowadays, the norm is for us to see a product designed in one country, produced in five, and marketed in 20 countries![76]

Addressing culture across a virtual organization. Organizations have steadily increased their use of the virtual workforce. In 2011, 563 North American firms were surveyed.[77] The results indicated that 37% of them employ full time teleworkers. In the survey, firms cited lower costs of operation as being the primary motivator in the move to a virtual workforce, but also strongly emphasized the need for addressing the cultural component by creating improved work/life balance, and providing leadership that is more attuned to the interpersonal needs of the employee.

In the virtual workspace, most cultural challenges tend to take the form of communication misunderstandings exacerbated by location and differences in time zones. Leaders must evolve to new level of collaboration, socialization, and communication since all three support the virtual leaders' ability to better inspire and motivate a virtual team.[78] Researchers stress that formal training for leaders should include cultural social cues in an anonymous environment, social protocol, and common culture values.

Addressing culture across companies. Addressing culture only in terms of international aspects falls short of viewing important topics such as social variations, diversity, power relations, and corporate nuances. This is especially true when corporations combine forces to create a larger, and sometimes behemoth, structure. In merging two or more companies the most important consideration comes down to evaluating differences in corporate management styles. Permitting each company to maintain their prior management style generally creates problems particularly if one culture uses a hierarchical approach and another thrives on consensus building.

A cultural reinvention can provide an opportunity for all employees to collaborate and offer opinions whether they are located in corporate offices or in the virtual workspace. This level of involvement can make the crossover to a redefined corporation more palatable for all concerned. Paying attention to other cultural dynamics such as conflict resolution, corporate communication, respectful discourse and acceptable behavior, and deadline and milestone management is crucial.[79]

Addressing diverse cultures. This element of the intercultural aspect of virtual leadership begins with valuing diversity. An invisible leader needs to understand that diversity is crucial to leveraging the full power of innovation within a virtual organization. Diversity brings with it diverse thinking. Research has demonstrated that teams with members who are all of the same mind perform worse than those of a diverse nature. This is because diversity leads the team to reflect on possibilities and perspectives that might otherwise be ignored.[80]

The intercultural environment requires analysis for any major corporate transition. The international level of acceptance of telework is driven to some extent by the economic wealth of the country. For example, housing conditions in Central American countries may not offer a room or square footage for staging an at-home work environment.[81] Additionally, the level of in-home internet service and acceptable bandwidth may hinder implementation of a virtual organization in other countries. Hence, prior to launching telework in a country, it is important to consider whether working virtually is logistically viable for the workforce in that country.

Addressing culture across the globe. One of the first and most obvious considerations is that of language which may include building a language infrastructure on top of the internet in order to improve both the use and access of existing language services and accelerate language services that can unite employees in communication.[82]

A second issue is relocating virtual employees to other countries. Aside from the logistics of the physical move for employees, offering training and development in the area of cultural intelligence can equip them with the cultural tools to help assimilate them into a new cultural environment. The establishment of a code of conduct for new international virtual employees can help them understand the cultural expectations in their new location.[83]

The third element speaks to a checklist of important considerations for both the virtual leaders and virtual employees. These include:

- the correct visa/work permit in the host country
- virtual employee's employment agreement reflecting the telecommuting arrangement, and host-country law
- delivery of pay and benefits
- home and/or office space
- infrastructure for the employee to work effectively from home

- compliance of the home office space with local health and safety rules

- data protection, security, and confidentiality

- host country licenses.[84]

The Takeaway

"While employers may provide equipment and technology to telecommuters, that doesn't mean there will be a good cultural fit."[85] Defining culture in a virtual workforce starts with defining and assessing your corporate and organizational culture. It means understanding and communicating your internal culture and orientation to your invisible employees. It also means creating an understanding of internal culture across organizations and in different countries. But most of all it means creating a viable culture that ensures that all virtual employees from various cultures feel valued, important, and trusted. It is with a focus on the virtual employee as an individual, improvements can occur in areas such as attendance, recruitment, retention, and morale.

Chapter 10

TECHNOLOGY: USING TECHNOLOGY TO BRING BACK THE VISUAL CONNECTION!

"Technology now allows people to connect anytime, anywhere, to anyone in the world, from almost any device. This is dramatically changing the way people work, facilitating 24/7 collaboration with colleagues who are dispersed across time zones, countries, and continents."

—Michael Dell, CEO of Dell

Writing a chapter on technology for invisible leaders, or for anyone for that matter, is like trying to hit a moving target! In fact, I believe this chapter will be virtually obsolete (lol) by the time this book makes it to print. Hence, an excuse for the next edition! Nonetheless, instead of focusing on software release numbers, I will try to place most of the emphasis on the benefits of technology as it relates to you, the invisible leader. Do any of you remember Windows 1.0 released on November 20, 1985 or PC DOS version 1.0 which supported only floppy disks in August

1981? For sure we won't go in that direction! Instead, we will examine the advancements in technology that have created the tools for improved leadership of the virtual workspace as a more connected workforce around the world.

The Story

This is my story about Frank. Frank occupied a C-level position in the federal IT arena in San Francisco and was very much interested in all things technology. In fact, everyone in our organization thought Frank did nothing but play with and test the latest and greatest toys of technology. The real irony, and the essence of this anecdote, resides in his belief system surrounding technology training.

Our organization was comprised of IT professionals who came to their jobs knowing a great deal about technology—at that time. As technology evolved, these very bright and hard-working employees needed to learn about the new software and applications that were coming into use. So now, here's the rub. Frank believed that if employees were designated as IT professionals, those people should take care of their training needs on an individual basis and at personal expense.

Needless to say, that didn't happen and Frank was eventually left with a technologically obsolete workforce. For those employees working virtually, this was an exceptionally difficult burden since access to team members was limited at the time, and the IT helpdesk (aka the IT helpless desk) was also woefully under-trained and became more so every day. By the time Frank retired, the technology side of the organization was essentially inept and leaving the organization to find new work. These people entered the organization as capable and current IT professionals working virtually, and left as administrative order takers!

Unfortunately, while Frank understood the technology and its power, he rarely used it with his virtual team and allowed his virtual workforce to whither on the technological vine. Frank failed to understand the impact of technology and the importance of keeping his invisible team technologically up to date.

The Theory

Extraordinary leaps in technology set the stage for a new work model. It has been said that, "Technological revolutions lead to people revolutions."[86] This is the case for technology and its impact on advancing the revolution in virtual work; and how work is performed in and out of the office. Over time, research has come to demonstrate that the shift to the virtual workplace involved much more than a blueprint for scaling technology; it has required a change strategy in leadership for those who work in the virtual space.

The collaborative side of technology. Obviously the richest method for collaboration is that of face-to-face communication. Since it brings us the leveraging power of eye contact, touch, voice, and body language it naturally offers deeper insight into the communication as well as the ability to evaluate the responses of others in terms of nonverbal cues. These are the cues that speak to professional intimacy and trust. Technologies such as texting, messaging, and email are considered to be lean since they don't offer these cues. However, technologies that provide the *human element* such as videoconferencing and video phone calls give the listener the ability to interpret tone, stress, facial expressions, and hand gestures.[87]

Your role as an invisible leader in creating a technology-driven virtual organization that achieves this is crucial and requires oversight to ensure that state-of-the-art technology is procured, implemented, and updated on an ongoing basis. The following technologies bring benefits that far exceed their costs.

Web or video conferencing. Since the intent of a message can be misinterpreted in email or texting, a communication plan should include a strong visual aspect such as web or video conferencing. We have all encountered situations with texting where our intent did not get communicated or where the receiver of the text was offended simply because the message seemed short and curt—even with emojis! Such is the nature of texting. However, where it is overused the messaging takes on a robotic flair. For invisible employees, this can easily lead them to feel unimportant. That perception, in and of itself, can impact productivity and employee retention. The feeling of connection where everyone is visually connected is truly *the next best thing to being there!*

Cloud computing and virtualization. Cloud technology drives access to files from remote locations so that virtual employees can perform their work anytime, anywhere, and from multiple devices.

The Virtual Private Network (VPN). A VPN reduces security issues for the teleworker. It provides a secure and private connection between the remote user and the office (or the cloud, or HQ . . .).

Collaborative software. In a world of innovation, the ability to collaborate is crucial. As Ken Blanchard said, "None of us is as smart as all of us." A few of the tools (from a seemingly endless array) that can assist the invisible leader to encourage teams collaborate and remain connected include the following.

- **Slack.** Slack can keep all team communication in one place.

- **Asana.** Asana tracks and organizes project work and enables discourse.

- **Yammer.** Yammer is a private social network that helps employees collaborate across departments, locations and business apps.

- **HipChat.** HipChat is a private hosted chat service designed to help teams collaborate more efficiently.

While there is no way to identify all of the collaborative software for enhancing peer-to-peer work in a virtual environment, the above serve as a few examples of the veritable buffet of products that can help the invisible workforce.[88]

The fun side of technology—gamification. Gamification has been shown to enhance productivity and reduce the degree to which virtual employees feel socially isolated. Through research of 69 teleworkers, whose average age was 41, results indicate that by using gamification (which included an avatar of the virtual employee) over a traditional approach of lecture training, the teleworkers were more intrinsically motivated to perform and to use the system than those who received traditional training. In addition, these virtual workers demonstrated an increase in individual productivity.[89]

Making the leap—the logistical side of the technology. Making the leap into the virtual workforce offers organizations the opportunity to upgrade their technology in terms of hardware, software, groupware, and video. Ultimately, transitions to leading-edge technologies will serve to improve productivity through enhanced system response time, improved organization of data, and collaborative methods of sharing information and developing innovative solutions for clients. Below are a few of the details that are integral to technology transition to the virtual organization.

- A Technology Division that provides the necessary hardware, software, groupware, secure cloud data repositories, and multi-site video conferencing capabilities
- Phased implementation that serves as the enabler of communication and work products that includes assessment, procurement, and configuration of the hardware and software
- A process of identifying equipment requirements and ordering
- A procurement plan that affords the organization opportunities for strategic sourcing to reduce costs
- Configuration that takes place in advance of transition of employees

- A just in time training plan to be concurrent with the arrival of the technology.

The Takeaway

As an invisible leader, you stand in the center of technology and must balance both social and communication interfaces which are intricate and difficult to manage.[90] Without deliberate and enhanced communication (i.e. teleconferencing, videoconferencing, groupware, email, social media, avatars, blogs, etc.) on the part of leadership, members of the virtual workforce can experience confusing and inaccurate messages. They can become disconnected from their team,[91] develop a sense of workplace isolation, suffer a loss of professional identity,[92] and acquire a disaffection for the organization as a whole.[93] As a result, virtual organizations are more intricate than office-based organizations and require leadership with greater emphasis on communication and focused teamwork.[94]

Part III

THE HOW-TO'S OF BECOMING A SUCCESSFUL INVISIBLE LEADER

Chapter 11

YOUR INVISIBLE
LEADERSHIP MODEL

The Invisible Leadership Model is comprised of four interdependent levels on a pyramid. Each level builds on the one beneath it and ultimately leads to a successful virtual organization. The model is grounded in creating the successful virtual organization by making invisible employees feel valued, important, and trusted.

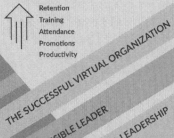

We already have discussed the first level of the model which is located at the base of the pyramid and addresses the influential dynamics of creating a successful virtual organization. These dynamics include the social, political, economic, legal, intercultural, and technology dynamics of creating a virtual organization. The dynamics lay the foundation for introducing transformational leadership into the virtual organization.

Transformational leadership is the style of leadership where leaders provide individualized consideration, intellectual stimulation, inspiration/motivation, and idealized influence to those they lead. The first two layers of the pyramid model exist to support the invisible leader. It is by addressing the influential dynamics and employing a transformational leadership style that ensures the invisible leader is positioned to create the successful virtual organization. The path to the successful virtual organization fuses the dynamics and leadership style through the following elements of leadership.

- Trust
- Encouragement
- Communication
- Recognition
- Rewards
- Care/concern
- Assessment
- Collaboration
- Listening

- Relating
- Training
- Engaging
- Developing
- Empowering
- Promoting
- Diversifying
- Feedback
- Team building
- Celebrating

As noted earlier, the successful virtual organization is an organization that maintains metrics better than or equal to that of its previous office environment. The metrics consist of employee productivity, retention, attendance, training, and promotions. When a virtual organization meets its numbers in these areas, both the organization and the leader are deemed successful and the virtual leader can actually sleep at night!

The four chapters that follow, address the dimensions of a transformational style. The dimensions of transformational leadership are generally referred to as the 4 I's (individualized consideration, intellectual stimulation, inspiration/motivation, and idealized influence). Let's take a look at the 4 I's as we delve into specific tactics and techniques to best implement transformational leadership in the virtual workspace.

Chapter 12

NICE MATTERS! SHOW THEM YOU GIVE A DAMN!

"I've learned that people will forget what you said, people will forget what you did, but people will never forget how you made them feel."

—*Maya Angelou*

Leading in the virtual workspace is not as easy as it sounds. At the start you may think that not having so many employees coming in and out of your office will almost be a Zen experience; so different from the revolving door of people with questions, concerns, and frustrations. Invisible employees do not offer a panacea to your seemingly never-ending interruptions. In fact, if you have this mindset, you may find yourself with an entirely different set of problems! The kind of problems where simple unanswered questions can turn into huge blunders; where concerns become larger business problems; and where frustrations resolve themselves with resignations of otherwise great employees. Putting your head in the sand and believing that just because you don't see your invisible employees, they don't need your attention is so wrong! In reality, they need **_more_** of your attention in a more mindful, conscientious, and consistent manner.

The Story

I am reminded of when I was an invisible employee working for an invisible leader. The invisible leader was Xavier, and he was a piece of work! Since I was working for him virtually, I rarely saw him. Xavier lived in San Francisco and I lived in San Diego, but that didn't keep him from being extraordinarily demanding and downright meanspirited when we did interact. And even though my organization had the highest productivity numbers on the west coast, his phone calls to me mostly concerned the most minute errors on my part or demands for me to work late. A call from Xavier, always meant something bad. Even though Xavier knew I was a single parent and that I had some personal challenges, never once did he ask how I was or if I was having a good day. He simply did not give a damn.

I recall once we were together on a trip to DC. The weather was horrendously bad. We should not have made the trip to begin with, but for Xavier (the consummate Type A personality and a perennial bull in a china shop) this was a must attend session with colleagues. When we arrived by taxi to the meeting site, we entered the meeting room and began to set up our computers. I was tasked with carrying all of the equipment (Xavier considered me his personal minion). Unfortunately, I left one extension cord (not really necessary for this meeting) back at the hotel. It was at this point that Xavier did something that I shall never forget. He sent me out into the freezing cold to find a taxi to go and "fetch" the extension cord back at the hotel. Please keep in mind there were plenty of extension cords in the building—all he had to do was request one! But no, he ordered me out into an unforgiving storm.

Needless to say, I waited for quite a while to get a cab. Cold, frazzled, and upset, I remained tenacious and finally accomplished what he had demanded I do—get the freaking extension cord! When I arrived back to the meeting, looking bedraggled and unkempt from the wind and snow, Xavier had already procured a cord and was moving along with the briefing. I don't think I need to tell you how I felt! Fortunately, things changed and eventually I was blessed with a new and wonderful leader who promoted me to a level equivalent to Xavier. I will never forget Xavier and I shall not say more!

The Theory—Individualized Consideration

Leadership in a virtual organization is the single factor that drives and determines the success of the organization[95] and a transformational leadership style is the way to get there. When invisible leaders commit to team members they are acknowledging the human and singularly most important element of the organization. So how does an invisible leader demonstrate true consideration for the invisible employee? Clearly, given the story I just shared, caring about people and being mindful of circumstances can go a long way especially on those rare occasions when the invisible leader and employee are together! However, most times invisible leadership is just that—invisible—and leaders need to leverage other forms of individualized consideration.

One way is through feedback and recognition. Critical to invisible leadership in virtual teams is feedback to individual team members.[96] This form of interaction can make virtual employees feel an integral part of the organization and reinforce a sense of connection to the organization. Since virtual employees do not have the benefit of frequent face-to-face interaction with leadership, we as virtual leaders need to offer early and frequent performance feedback. In addition, virtual employees need to be included in succession planning so that they understand they are being recognized for their work in the context of promotion and career advancement. Research shows that rewards and recognition are integral to the success of the virtual team.[97]

Another way the invisible leader demonstrates care and concern for the virtual employee is through trust. In 2003 when approximately 20% of the workforce participated in some form of telework, a study of 29 virtual workforce teams showed that leaders of teams with the highest levels of trust were the most productive. These teams shared the following characteristics: they started their interactions on a social basis creating a positive team dynamic; they defined clear roles for the team members; and they maintained a positive attitude.[98] According to this research, building trusting relationships in virtual organizations is even more important than in face-to-face organizations.

Empowerment is the third way an invisible leader shows individualized consideration for virtual employees. Empowerment can be viewed as allowing others to lead themselves. It is the empowering leader who creates an organization of responsibility, initiative, and confidence.[99] This aspect of invisible leadership permits virtual employees the latitude to make decisions related to their own work. For effective empowerment, guidelines are created and include; setting the vision, communicating, ensuring feedback, engaging the organization, collaborating, and providing for the growth and development of the team. The overall intent is to ensure that team members see themselves as important employees as well as valued, trusted, and empowered partners.[100]

If empowering employees causes you to think "... it's bad enough I can't see my people, now I have to empower them as well?" You are not alone! Managers, in general, have difficulty dealing with a loss of control especially considering that these managers must remain accountable for the bottom line.

Perhaps surprising is that there is actually an ROI to be had by empowering virtual employees! One of these benefits is an overall increase in productivity. Employees who feel empowered tend to value their position more and actually produce more. Another benefit is an increase in job satisfaction. Oftentimes, empowered employees come to think and act more like business owners rather than employees. Feeling the sense of empowerment can generate a strong sense of autonomy and ownership.

So at this point you may be asking, how do I specifically create individualized consideration and make my invisible employees feel valued, important, and trusted? There are four actions that can lay the groundwork for doing this.

Listening. Individualized consideration lies in listening, making deliberate contact with your invisible employees, and driving conversation so that you can hear out their ideas and their concerns. However, the secret sauce lies in taking action on their input. This will assure them that even though they are not working in the same venue as you, that you trust and value their input, and that they are an important and integral part of your team.[101]

My intent in sharing this is not to paint a picture where things are rosy and perfect 100% of the time. Sometimes your invisible employees may need to offer a negative commentary. And sometimes you will need to do the same! This is where having built a relationship founded on individualized consideration really pays off. If you make the effort to build a strong and trusting relationship, and you need to share negative feedback, your odds of that feedback being accepted in a positive manner have increased. Consider this, would you rather take *constructive* criticism (is there really such a thing?) from a person you trust or someone you hardly know? If you only make contact with an invisible employee when times are bad, future contacts with that employee will come with a negative connotation.

Getting to know your invisible employees. If you really want your invisible employees to feel valued, make the effort to get to know them on a person-to-person basis. Sales people have the relationship business down to a science! Each day they try to learn more and more about their clients on a personal basis. They touch base with clients to talk about family, sports, and how they spent the weekend. And they reciprocate by sharing their own personal information. Truly getting to know your virtual employees works in much the same way. Hence, it is vital that you put forth the effort to get to know your virtual employees on a professional and personal basis. Take the time to ask them about family members, the kinds of things they like to do when they are not working, and even what they like or dislike about their jobs. Showing a personal interest makes these employees feel less like a cog in corporate machinery and more like vital and valued individuals.[102]

Being approachable. Since communication is a two-way street, it is important that your invisible employees feel comfortable contacting you to ask questions, field ideas, and request help. Keep in mind though you may not have all of the answers to their questions;

- you can use the situation to be helpful in finding the answers

- your honesty in saying "I don't know" can garner the respect and loyalty of your employees

- you can give them the opportunity to be part of creating the solution allowing them to feel a more integral part of your organization.[103]

This means that you not only make yourself approachable, but that you are responsive as well. All too often, invisible leaders fail to respond to calls and emails from their virtual employees in a timely manner, leaving them to feel ignored and unimportant. My personal metric for responsiveness is two hours. Even if my response will take longer than two hours to create, I still respond within two hours to let people know that I am researching an answer.

Providing the human touch. Offering respect and appreciation for a job well-done is not a sign of weakness, nor will it position your invisible employees to take advantage of your kindness. A stern façade is not what it takes to garner the respect of your invisible employees, and demonstrating an emotional side is not weakness. Your positive emotional side is exactly what creates a happy and motivated team. Sometimes, leaders are concerned that they might be seen as a *soft touch* and that they might be *played*. In actuality, displaying your human side will create an environment where your virtual team will work harder and admire you more![104]

The Takeaway

Individualized consideration in transformational leadership amounts to having concern and caring for invisible employees. What this boils down to is *be yourself*. Think of the golden rule and treat your virtual employees as you would like to be treated; with respect, transparency, and trust.[105] Acting otherwise, risks damaging relationships and losing employees. Invest the extra time and effort it takes to achieve this in the virtual environment. It is incumbent upon you, the invisible leader, to pay attention to cues in voice and the written word to pick up on the nuances that may indicate your invisible employee is having a bad day. On a daily basis, ask yourself if you are letting your virtual employees know that you give a damn! Remember, it's your job to make your invisible employees feel valued, important, and trusted.

Chapter 13

TRAIN 'EM AND THEY MIGHT LEAVE, DON'T TRAIN 'EM AND THEY MIGHT STAY!

"Train people well enough so they can leave, treat them well enough so they don't want to."

—*Richard Branson*

Research finds that in spite of what we may have come to believe, salary is not the primary key to employee engagement and happiness! In fact, the real driver comes down to intellectual stimulation and is valued three times as much as money.[106] This is especially true for virtual employees who rely on the essence of their jobs to drive their engagement. And so we ponder, how does an invisible leader provide for intellectual stimulation on the job?

The Story

This is the story of Norm. For decades Norm had avoided the spotlight, especially when it came to public speaking. Norm had never traveled away from his home office in Oakland, California. At one point our organization took on a nationwide initiative to provide a new service offering to our sister organizations across the country. Now it's important to keep in mind that our *sisters* weren't particularly open to using our service! So we were trying to sell to an unwilling marketplace. This meant that my invisible team needed to connect with invisible customers. Fundamentally, this required that everyone get on the campaign trail and visit and speak to large groups of potential clients. For Norm, this was going to be worse than death!

I must admit that Norm and I had many conversations concerning his fear and perturbations about public speaking. However, the time came for a full court press on preparing Norm emotionally and professionally for the "dreaded" task that lie ahead of him. We had more dry-runs, practice sessions, and pep talks than anyone could imagine! Finally, the day came when Norm traveled to give his first briefing. The group was only about 25 people, but Norm handled the presentation as if he was speaking to 2500! He was calm, self-assured, and the audience hung on his every word—it was as if EF Hutton was speaking! Everyone listened and gave Norm the most glowing reviews—and then they did business with us!

After his first speech, there was no stopping Norm. The assignments were intellectually stimulating for him and he became our #1 go to person for public speaking. It's now years later and Norm is still leading the charge presenting in the public forum arena. Norm rocks!

The Theory—Intellectual Stimulation

It is important to note that intellectual stimulation goes well beyond a single project or task. It is the overall combination of training, development and assignments that are exciting and fun for the invisible employee. Unfortunately, invisible employees are often forgotten when training and development opportunities are available. They frequently miss out on impromptu in-office planning sessions. They are forgotten when funds become available for formal university courses. And they are rarely given the plum projects! Nonetheless, when it comes to intellectual stimulation there are a number of straight-forward steps to follow.

Provide autonomy. Autonomy goes well beyond empowerment, it provides invisible employees a sense of freedom and a way to self-determine how to plan, handle, and address projects and assignments. For example, the worker can create personal goals to achieve workload milestones, and adjust scheduling to achieve those milestones.[107]

Ensure opportunity for feedback. This step begins with assignments that are interesting and challenging. Literature indicates that one of the most often overlooked elements of positive leadership in virtual teams is feedback to individual team members in the form of challenging assignments coupled with recognition to make virtual employees feel important to the organization. Since virtual employees do not have the benefit of frequent face-to-face interaction with leadership, feedback and recognition tell invisible employees that they are valued members of the team.[108]

Provide training and development. Training and development can be on the job as well as in a formal educational setting. Research points to a need to provide for career development through training plans that are specifically designed for the virtual worker.[109] Nonetheless, the lack of professional development is a huge cause of concern among virtual workers as they can easily be passed over for training and promotion since they lack corporate visibility.[110] In fact, invisible employees indicate they are being held back from promotions because their leadership did not coach them or create a definitive development plan.

The Takeaway

The overall result of intellectual stimulation is that leaders who remain mindful of the important role invisible workers play in their organization with satisfying assignments and appropriate rewards and recognition are more likely to retain these employees.[111] Offering appropriate autonomous assignments help create engaged virtual employees. Providing feedback, rewards, and recognition reinforce the importance of the invisible employee to the organization. And providing training and development to take them to the next level in the organization serve to help keep invisible employees from wandering off to another employer. Such actions help contribute to the overall success of your invisible organization.

Chapter 14

ORDER LESS AND INSPIRE MORE!

"People often say that motivation doesn't last. Well, neither does bathing. That's why we recommend it daily."

−Zig Ziglar

Do you wake each workday revved up and ready to get to work? You may very likely wake up thinking about money (more than 50% of us do), but research tells us that the role of the leader directly influences our motivation to work; essentially saying that our leaders need to be our motivators.[112] This is especially true in the virtual workspace. If the invisible leader is toxic, the motivation to get to work, let alone do a good job, is diminished. Similarly, the opposite occurs when you serve as a motivational source—job satisfaction increases, stress is relieved, and your virtual employees are less prone to hit the snooze button!

The Story

One of my favorite stories is about Francine. Francine led an off-site proposal team for a defense contractor for an extremely large and lucrative deal. The proposal took nearly a year and Francine worked tirelessly seven days a week and 10+ hours per day. At the end of the project everyone on the team was exhausted and especially Francine since she balanced a family that included three children with her work. Shortly after the proposal was completed a large box arrived at Francine's home addressed to her children. The box was filled with toys and a note that read, "Thank you for sharing your mom with us this past year. She did a great job!" I don't know if Francine ever came down from the joy of that moment. Francine was over-the-moon inspired and motivated to work for this leader and remained with the organization for many years to come.

The Theory—Inspirational Motivation

Given economic challenges and an evolving virtual workforce, leaders are beset by the need to innovate with respect to their overall style of leadership where organizations are flatter and the workforce almost demands a say in decisions.[113] In general, invisible leaders face a less controllable environment and must adapt by offering a voice to their employees; simply put, they must order less and inspire more.

Acting as an inspirationally motivating role model for employees is clearly one of the most important functions of the leader. When hundreds of miles separate an invisible leader from employees, the leader does not have the latitude to go out with the team after work for a few beers and share what is happening on the political front and what that might mean to their organization. Instead, the invisible leader must share information, usually voice to voice while attempting to recognize and interpret vocal body language. This means paying extra attention to intonation, pauses in speech, and emphasis used in vocal communication. Inspiring and motivating invisible employees presents the biggest challenge—keeping them *amped* to do their jobs while feeling enthusiastic and driven. Research underscores that invisible leaders must evolve to a new level of collaboration, socialization, and communication since all three support the virtual leader's ability to better inspire and motivate a virtual team.[114]

There are a number of specific ways to provide ongoing inspiration and motivation using technology and perhaps the best way to start is with a simple "Good Morning!".[115] When you physically walk into the office in the morning, don't you say good morning to everyone? Then why wouldn't you say that to your invisible employees? A quick and easy "good morning" instant message tells your virtual team you think of them, you value them, and you have not forgotten about them! This straightforward action can go a long way to inspire and motivate your team in the hinterlands!

According to *Incentive*, other ways to insert a dose of inspiration and motivation is through the following actions and activities.[116]

- *Weekly recognition conference calls.* Even a simple "great job with that proposal" can do wonders for the employee who stayed up half the night to get the job done.

- *Monthly face to face sessions either in person or online.* If financially possible, bring the team into the office periodically to share ideas and build relationships. This can occur virtually as well as with brainstorming sessions, respectful discourse, and even games.

- *Daily electronic updates using visual technology.* These communications can keep everyone up to speed on the corporate and organizational front. They also can create a community of practice and trusting space for chatting and sharing both work and non-work information.

- *Making birthdays important.* Even invisible employees have birthdays! Make the day special by offering the day off with pay.

- *Don't forget the non-technology!* Sometimes the old-fashioned hand-written thank you note or phone call can create an inspiring workday for the invisible employee.

- *Be culturally intelligent.* Remain aware that your invisible team may be composed of diverse cultures. Take time to study the various cultures represented on your team. Learn the nuances of holidays from culture to culture.

The Takeaway

Simply put, you need to order less and inspire more! By finding ways to interact more, you can bridge the gap between you and your invisible worker. Since it is all too easy to get bogged down by what is happening in the office, you will need to work to find reasons to connect with your virtual employees. Start by sending out positive mirror neurons with "Good Morning" messages, calendaring weekly calls, celebrating milestones (both business and personal—birthdays, marriages, new babies, etc.), and organizational successes. Inspire, motivate, and reap the benefits. If you think your virtual employees are important, so will they!

Chapter 15

WHERE'S YOUR CHARISMA?

"How can you have charisma? Be more concerned about making others feel good about themselves than you are making them feel good about you."
— Dan Reiland—Former Partner, John Maxwell

Charisma is a mysterious charm or personality or even magnetism. Some people think you either have it or you don't. But, charisma has components and characteristics that all of us should nurture. Characteristics include sensitive and communicative body language, optimism, poised confidence, even a friendly smile and an assuring voice. No matter how you view it, in leadership, charisma is that *je ne sais quoi* (that certain something!) that can give you incredible leverage to influence those you lead. As an invisible leader, it takes focus and work to share your charisma with your invisible employees.

The Story

This is the story of David—no, not the one from the Bible! David was a leader of mine who worked on the East Coast and wielded more influence in our DC organization than I have ever seen.

David was attractive, articulate, friendly with all levels of the organization and perhaps most importantly, *in the know*. David's knowledge and understanding of what might impact our organization was amazing and what made us idolize him more was that he was willing to share his insights as to what could affect all of us in the future. David was quick to go to bat for any of his invisible employees to get us promoted or obtain additional training for us.

I recall one time in particular during a change in the political administration when David realized that our nationwide organization might be impacted by a strong downsizing effort. Playing strategically, David prepared us for the data calls and justifications we would have to put forth if the organization would continue to exist. Sure enough, when the hammer came down to inspect our organization, we had a full and complete rationale ready for the inspection team and we soared through the evaluation with flying colors. Had it not been for David, we would have become just another statistic in the list of obliterated *officialdoms!*

The Theory—Idealized Influence

Idealized influence is defined in terms of charisma, motivation, and consideration towards employees.[117] It is through your personal style and charisma that you can instill loyalty and commitment to you and to your organization. Exuding charisma is the key to unlocking, instilling, and nurturing the core aspect of your organizational mission. As an invisible leader, your charisma serves to create pride, respect, and trust on the part of your followers.[118]

But there's more! Your idealized influence goes farther and results in a sense of confidence on the part of your invisible employees; giving them the ability to accept and adapt to future changes in your organization.[119] As a result you must work more diligently to develop relationships with your invisible employees.[120] Ultimately, the key to idealized leadership is using influence on a social level to create new attitudes and behaviors for the team.[121]

Employees tend to follow leaders because they sense a special *it* (charisma) in their leaders. They find it both attracting and mesmerizing. And though you may believe charisma is a trait of only well-known leaders, research tells us that it is 50% innate and 50% learned.[122] So in pursuing the learned side of charisma, let's take a look at ingredients that can generate and revitalize your idealized influence.[123]

Confidence. Charismatic leaders possess a strong sense of self and exude confidence. Consider this; you are about to step on to a flight. Obviously the leader of the flight is the pilot. You respectfully say hello and say, "... how are you this fine day?" What if the pilot responds with. "... um, I really don't think it's a great day to fly." How do you feel about going on the flight with this pilot? Right!!! You are ready to bolt and find another flight with another pilot!

Similarly, an invisible leader can easily lose employees if a sense of confidence does not come through. Overall, the confident leader is one that retains passenger-followers in the organization. Leader confidence needs to come through in the virtual space—even during the tough times! That's why your communication in all forms needs to exude your confidence; in your voice body language, in your intonation, in your online facial expressions, and in your writing. If you are not confident in yourself, how can you expect your invisible team to be confident in you?

Creativity. The most charismatic and influential leaders are out-of-the-box thinkers. They are willing to take appropriate risks, and they drive innovation. If you can see opportunity when a problem comes up, you are well on your way to idealized influence! In the virtual space, creative leaders create the springboard for their invisible employees to be creative since they model the stance for effective innovation.

Vision. Research indicates that 41% of executives look for the ability in future leaders to empower employees to execute to a vision. For your role as an invisible leader, sharing and effectively communicating the vision is crucial. Your virtual employees need to fully understand your vision if they are to execute it. Simon Sinek wrote "Leadership requires two things: a vision of the world that does not yet exist and the ability to communicate it". You have a vision, now communicate it to your invisible employees!

Your Interest in Others. Your ability to ask pertinent questions is critical to engaging invisible employees. For example, ask what one thing fascinates them about their job and find out why. As you converse, address people by name and do it frequently. References such as *he* or *she* lack a personable approach. When you speak, speak with a warm voice and when on video, smile, smile, smile!!!

The Takeaway

Be yourself. The invisible leader who is disingenuous can be spotted a mile, or a half a globe away. Speaking honestly can create the kind of influence you need and will rely on as the months and years tick by. By being confident and optimistic that the future is bright allows you to leverage your influence in a positive manner. After all, who wants to fly with a pilot who thinks it is a bad day to be in the air!

Being creative and willing to think outside the box will allow and encourage your invisible workforce to also think creatively without fear of offering a new idea or *coloring outside of the lines.* Similarly, share your vision openly and freely and allow your invisible team to offer additional ideas. Above all, be interested in your invisible team!

Part IV

THE FINAL TAKEAWAYS

THE INVISIBLE LEADERSHIP MODEL

Creating a Successful Virtual Organization by Making Invisible Employees Feel Valued, Important, and Trusted

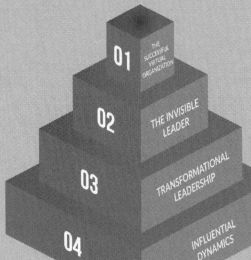

Chapter 16

THE FINALE

"May you live in interesting times."

—*Chinese Proverb*

Seeing the invisible workforce take shape has been more than interesting. Employees no longer need to be hitched to a desk and chair in a corporate office since work and collaboration can occur anytime and from any place—from church on Sunday or while listening to a long-winded high school commencement speech. And while the presence of virtual work has become more pervasive, the need to examine the factors that define and impact a successful virtual organization has become increasingly important.

Hence, the need to focus on leadership and the components of a successful virtual organization are important. Overall, factors that define a successful virtual organization are metrics greater than or equal to in-person organizations in terms of employee productivity, retention, attendance, professional development, and upward mobility. Unfortunately, all too often virtual leaders do not navigate very well through the challenges associated with guiding a virtual workforce, and find their virtual teams do not achieve predetermined metrics and are deemed failures.[124] In fact, less than half of telework situations succeed due to inexpert leadership.[125] The fact is that virtual projects and employees are more likely to fail if leaders employ the same leadership traits at the same levels for the virtual workforce that they use for co-located employees.[126] So if you are losing sleep at night as you worry about your virtual organization and whether it can succeed, it is for good reason. Your virtual organization can easily fail and if it does, you will go down with it!

If you are losing sleep at night worrying that your virtual organization will not meet its numbers this is the book you want! This book prescribes a leadership model you need to eliminate your concerns about lower productivity, employee attrition, employee absences, and lack of employee growth and promotions. The significance of this book is that well-executed, invisible leadership where invisible employees feel valued, important, and trusted is the solution to improved metrics and uninterrupted sleep for you.

The first overarching issue that surfaced in this book indicated that invisible leaders need developmental training in virtual leadership. The core of the issue is that virtual leaders need to learn and understand that leading invisible workers is unique from leading employees who are co-located and within a leader's field of vision. Invisible leaders need to learn how to ensure that their employs do not feel unappreciated or viewed as second-class employees. As the saying goes, ". . . a person who feels appreciated will always do more than what is expected."[127]

For those invisible leaders who remain skeptical about having virtual employees, think again! Training/development on the topics of social cues in an anonymous environment, social protocol, and the art of creating common culture values across a virtual enterprise is a must. For you, this means taking stock of your views and perceptions of invisible employees and possibly looking into training and development programs that will help you become the consummate invisible leader.

The second and perhaps the more significant concept in this book is that leaders of virtual organizations need to focus on leading virtual employees **_more_** than they do in-office employees. Unfortunately, all too often, invisible employees experience a decline in leadership as they began working as virtual employees. Hence, it is important that virtual leaders make adjustments in their leadership behaviors to accommodate the distance factors of time and space, and ramp up their leadership style and efforts.

So, what's next? What's a leader to do or not do to achieve a successful virtual organization? What should you begin doing or continuing to do? Start with positive actions. The invisible leader needs to care about employees as individuals by trusting, empowering, and recognizing them; by assigning them purposeful work, providing them constructive feedback, encouraging their professional growth; and by providing them visibility throughout the organization. Positive actions set the stage for enhanced productivity, and greater employee retention for an ongoing successful virtual organization. These are positive actions you can take to engage and keep your virtual employees.

- Provide clear and frequent communication.

- Reach out to virtual workers to find out how they are doing on a personal level.

- Have discussions with individual employees regarding their future aspirations.

- Assist with plans to help virtual workers achieve their professional and personal goals.

- Encourage employees to develop new subject matter expertise.

- Provide leadership development.

- Provide funding and time off for professional growth.

- Create an organizational social media site to help socialize the team.

- Permit and encourage virtual employees to rotate and take the lead in meetings.

- Assign purposeful projects to employees that offer visibility up the management chain.

- Empower workers to design and execute projects in an autonomous manner.

- Encourage an open-door policy of communication and be responsive when they reach out to you.

- Ask for opinions and ideas where virtual workers see they are making welcomed suggestions to solving organizational challenges.

- Advocate and support brainstorming via video conferencing to provide a venue for innovation.

- Schedule teleconferences that are content rich where all virtual employees are given a chance to share their thoughts in an environment where their contributions are valued.

- Allow for time during status calls for virtual workers to share their highs and lows of the previous week.

- Create informal chat rooms and communities of practice to engage virtual workers to offer solutions, ideas, and opinions before final project decisions are made.

- Discuss the meaning and context of activities at headquarters.

- Employ individual Skype chats to underscore a respectful personal connection.

- Personalize rewards—flowers, family gift cards for dinner/movie, etc.

- Formally recognize virtual workers.

- Fund nominal peer-to-peer awards.

- And last but not least—leaders should be assessed before and during assignments to ensure suitability for their invisible roles.

And if all of these positive actions aren't enough, below is a list of negative behaviors that you should remove from your repertoire.

- Infrequent and unclear communication.
- Micro-management.

- Disrespect/calling out mistakes of employees during meetings or in front of other employees.
- Reluctance to train and mentor.[128]

So what does the future hold? While the projections for an increase in the virtual workforce worldwide vary widely, virtually all accounts anticipate continued growth trends. Ultimately, the future of successful virtual organizations rests on a reorientation of leadership towards a transformational style. This will require a virtual leadership style that anchors itself on individualized consideration, and humanizes virtual employees beyond the role of automatons; a style that cares for and has concern for virtual employees as individuals. It will require a focus on intellectual stimulation in the form of ongoing development with work assignments that allow virtual workers to stretch and grow as well as training and development programs that take employees to the next level of their professions. It will require charismatic leaders to exercise more idealized influence as well as inspiration and motivation towards virtual employees than they do towards workers who work down the hall. A transition to transformational leadership will set the stage for more successful virtual organizations in the future.

Overall, this book sheds a light on the need for leadership development; one that is focused specifically on leaders of virtual organizations. It also sends a message that invisible leaders need to lead their virtual workers _more_ than they lead their in-office employees. In addition, this book captures specific leadership behaviors inherently necessary for virtual leadership as a combination of behaviors that focus on human concern, trust, empowerment, recognition, and mentoring of virtual employees. But most importantly this book offers the secret to creating and sustaining a successful virtual organization. The secret rests on making invisible people feel valued, important, and trusted. My hope is that this book brings you closer to the truly successful and authentic virtual leader you are meant to be and that you are able to sleep comfortably knowing that your "numbers" are being met!

Chapter 17

THE LEADER ASSESSMENT: ARE YOU READY FOR INVISIBLE LEADERSHIP?

Questionnaire

Using a scale of 0 to 10, please rate your leadership of virtual employees—with 0 reflecting the lowest rating and 10 reflecting the highest rating (whole numbers only). If you currently lead a virtual organization, with regard to virtual employees, preface each question below with the following, *How well do I.* If you are currently not a leader of a virtual organization, with regard to virtual employees, preface each question with *How much will I.*

1. trust, empower, and have concern for employees?

2. acknowledge employees via feedback and recognition?

3. be aware of the complexity and time necessary to complete projects that I assign?

4. support the development of employees through training, leadership, and certification programs?

5. discuss long-term plans for promotions in the organization?

6. fend off last minute assignments and data calls?

7. share the successes of employees to the hierarchy of the organization?

8. influence political forces to obtain meaningful projects?

9. obtain funding for training?

10. ensure I am politically positioned within to obtain promotions for my workers?

11. ensure I am financially positioned to meet expenses?

12. meet expenses for retaining good employees?

13. meet the costs associated with short or long term absences of employees?

14. ensure I am positioned to meet the costs associated with training?

15. prepare to meet the costs associated with promotions?

16. know the ergonomic requirements for employees?

17. know the regulations for dealing with a hostile working environment in a virtual organization?

18. be aware of the possible misinterpretation of your communication and messaging?

19. know the HR requirements for job development regarding counseling, designing, and approving training plans?

20. be aware of how to fairly assign high-visibility projects to virtual employees?

21. be aware of other-than-electronic communication to interface with the various cultures within your virtual organization?

22. address the intra/inter cultural differences among employees relating to showing respect?

23. encourage creative input across diverse employees?

24. implement training programs for employees concerning diversity and culture?

25. coach and mentor across the cultures of teams?

26. understand how important state-of-the-art technology is for employees?

27. provide high-level visibility throughout the organization for employees via state-of-the-art video technology?

28. understand the importance of secure and reliable technology support?

29. make technology training available?

30. cross-train employees using technology?

Answer Sheet

Enter your ratings for the questions and add the ratings for the rows and columns. Also provide a super-total for the answers of all 30 questions.

	Productivity	Retention	Attendance	Training	Promotions	TOTALS
Social	1.	2.	3.	4.	5.	
Political	6.	7.	8.	9.	10.	
Economic	11.	12.	13.	14.	15.	
Legal	16.	17.	18.	19.	20.	
Intercultural	21.	22.	23.	24.	25.	
Technological	26.	27.	28.	29.	30.	
TOTALS						

Analysis

Column subtotals. The following grid analyzes your virtual leadership score. The column subtotals give you an idea of how well-suited you are to lead your invisible organization to success.

- The total of the 1st column indicates your potential impact on employee productivity.

- The total of the 2nd column indicates your potential impact on employee retention.

- The total of the 3rd column indicates your potential impact on employee attendance.

- The total of the 4th column indicates your potential impact on employee training.

- The total of the 5th column indicates your potential impact on employee promotions.

Analysis of scores for each column:

- 45-60—you have a strong capacity to lead virtually in the associated area.

- 35-44—you should receive some training in the associated area.

- 25-34—you should receive significant virtual leadership development.

- 0-24—you are likely unsuited or not positioned to lead virtually.

Row subtotals. The row subtotals address your influential dynamics for leading invisibly.

- The total of the 1st row indicates your adaptability to the social nature of invisible leadership.

- The total of the 2nd row indicates your adaptability to the political nature of invisible leadership.

- The total of the 3rd row indicates your adaptability to the economic nature of invisible leadership.

- The total of the 4th row indicates your adaptability to the legal nature of invisible leadership.

- The total of the 5th row indicates your adaptability to the intercultural nature of invisible leadership.

- The total of the 6th row indicates your adaptability to the technological nature of invisible leadership.

  - 35-50—you have the influential dynamics to lead virtually

  - 25-34—you should receive some training in the associated area

  - 15-24—you should receive significant virtual leadership developmental training

  - 0-14—you are most likely unsuited or not positioned to lead virtually

Super Total. The super total of reported ratings gives you an assessment of how well-suited you are across the organizational dynamics to lead virtually.

- 240-300—you are well-suited to lead virtually

- 180-239—you should receive virtual leadership development

- 0-179—you are unlikely to have the inclination or predisposition to lead virtually and should participate in a long-term virtual leadership development program.

NOTES/REFERENCES

1   Nilles, J. (2013). *Teleworkable organizations*. Retrieved from http://www.jalahq.com/blog/2013/08/teleworkable-organizations/

2   Schmieder-Ramirez, J. & Mallette, L.A. (2007). *The SPELIT Power Matrix*. North Charleston, S.C.: Book Surge.

3   Global Workforce Analytics. (2017). 2017 State of Telecommuting in the U.S. Employee Workforce. http://global workplaceanalytics.com/2017-state-of-telecommuting-in-the-us

4   Chronos Consulting. (2011). *The state of virtual team utilization in the 21st century: A research survey.* Retrieved from http://www.chronosconsulting.org/dl/Virtual-Teams-Utilization-Research-Survey-Sep-1-2011.pdf

5   Tuuti, C. (2012, January, 23). 2012:The rise of the virtual workforce. *Federal Computer Week.* Retrieved from http://fcw.com/articles/2012/01/15/feat-watch-list-management-workforce.aspx

6   Snyder, K. (2012). Enhancing telework—A guide to virtual leadership. *The Public Manager.* Retrieved from http://www.astd.org/Publications/Magazines/The-Public-Manager/

Archives/2012/Spring/Enhancing-Telework-a-Guide-to-Virtual-Leadership

7   Golden, T. D., & Froman, A. (2011). Does it matter where your manager works? Comparing managerial work mode (traditional, telework, virtual) across subordinate work experiences and outcomes. *Human Relations.* 64(11), 1451-1475. doi:10.1177/0018726711418387

8   Elsbach, K. D., Cable, D. M., & Sherman, J. W. (2010). How passive 'face time' affects perceptions of employees: Evidence of spontaneous trait inference. *Human Relations.* 63(6), 735-760. doi:10.1077/0018726709353139

9   Snyder, K. (2012). Enhancing telework—A guide to virtual leadership. *The Public Manager.* Retrieved from http://www.astd.org/Publications/Magazines/The-Public-Manager/Archives/2012/Spring/Enhancing-Telework-a-Guide-to-Virtual-Leadership

10   Chronos Consulting. (2011). *The state of virtual team utilization in the 21st century: A research survey.* Retrieved from http://www.chronosconsulting.org/dl/Virtual-Teams-Utilization-Research-Survey-Sep-1-2011.pdf

11   Maruyama, T., & Tietze, S. (2012). From anxiety to assurance: Concerns and outcomes of telework. *Emerald.* 41(4), 450-469. doi:10.1108/00483481211229375

12   Rafter, M. (2011, November). Out of site. *Benefits Magazine,* 51.

13 Robertson, M., & Vink, P. (2012). Examining new ways of office work between the Netherlands and the USA. *Work*, 41, 5086-5090. doi:10.3233/WOR-2012-1042-5086

14 Shin, L. (2016). At These 125 Companies, All Or Most Employees Work Remotely. Forbes. https://www.forbes.com/sites/laurashin/2016/03/31/at-these-125-companies-all-or-most-employees-work-remotely/#3fb623956530

15 Yu, S. (2008, December). How to make teleworking work: Widespread adoption of telecommuting programs is often hindered by non-technical factors. *Communication News*, 30-32.

16 Gajendran, R. S., & Harrison, D. A. (2007). The good, the bad, and the unknown about telecommuting: Meta-analysis of psychological mediators and the individual consequences. *Journal of Applied Psychology*. 92(6), 1524-1541. doi:10.1037/0021-9010.92.6.1524

17 Mulki, J., Nardhi, F., Laddek, F., & Nanavaty-Dahl, J. (2009). Set up remote workers to thrive. *MIT Sloan Management Review*. Retrieved from http://sloanreview.mit.edu/article/set-up-remote-workers-to-thrive/

18 Cole, A. (2012, May 30). Retaining young feds takes finesse. *Federal Computer Week*, 15.

19 Almer, E. D., & Kaplan, S. E. (2002). The effects of flexible work arrangements on stressors, burnout, and behavioral job outcomes in public accounting. *Behavior Research in Accounting*, 14(1), 1-34. doi:10.2308/bria.2002.14.1.1

20 Noonan, M. C., & Glass, J. L. (2012). The hard truth about telecommuting. *Monthly Labor Review.* 38-45. Retrieved from http://www.bls.gov/opub/mlr/2012/06/art3full.pdf

21 Cooper, C. D., & Kurland, N. B. (2002). Telecommuting, professional isolation, and employee development in public and private organizations. *Journal of Organizational Behavior.* 23, 511-532. doi:10.1002/job.145

22 Nafukho, F. M., Graham, C.M., & Muyia, H.M.A. (2010). Harnessing and optimal utilization of human capital in virtual workplace environments. *Advances in Developing Human Resources,* 12(6), 648-664. doi:10.1177/1523422310394791

23 Solomon, C. M. (2000, May). Don't forget your telecommuters. *Workforce,* 56-61

24 Ferrazzi, K. (2012). Evaluating the Employees You Can't See. *Harvard Business Review.* https://hbr.org/2012/12/evaluating-the-employees-you-c

25 Offstein, E. H., & Morwock, J. M. (2009). *Making telework work.* Boston, MASS: Davies-Black.

26 Goleman, D. (2006). *Social intelligence.* New York, NY: Bantam Dell.

27 Ibid.

28 Peters, P., den Dulk, L., & De Ruijter, J. (2010). Equality, diversity and inclusion: An international journal. *Emerald Article,* 29(5) 517-531. doi:10.1108/0261015011052799

29 Kanter, R. M. (2001). Power, leadership, and participatory management. *Theory Into Practice.* 20(4), 219-224

30 Brown, H., Poole, M. S., & Rodgers, T. L. (2004). Interpersonal traits, complementarity, and trust in virtual collaboration. *Journal of Management Information Systems,* 20(4), 115-137.

31 Walinskas, K. (2012). Telework and virtual team leadership. *Business Know How.* Retrieved from http://www.business knowhow.com/manage/telework.htm

32 Sims, H. P., Faraj, S., & Yun, S. (2009) When should a leader be directive or empowering? How to develop your own situational theory of leadership. *Business Horizons,* 52(2), 149-158. doi:10.1016/j.bushor.2008.10.002

33 Bens, I. (2007). The ten essential processes of facilitative leaders. *Global Business & Organizational Excellence,* 26(5), 38-56. doi:10.1002/joe.20163

34 Kanter, R. M. (2001). Power, leadership, and participatory management. *Theory Into Practice.* 20(4), 219-224

35 Cascio, W., & Shurygailo, S. (2003). E-leadership and virtual teams. *Organizational Dynamics,* 31(4), 362-376.

36 Sims, H. P., Faraj, S., & Yun, S. (2009) When should a leader be directive or empowering? How to develop your own situational theory of leadership. *Business Horizons,* 52(2), 149-158. doi:10.1016/j.bushor.2008.10.002

37   Ibid

38   Leonard, B. (2011, June). Managing virtual teams. *HR Magazine,* 39-42.

39   Andrades, D. (2018). *Learning to pivot.* USA, Self-Published.

40   Mulki, J., Nardhi, F., Laddek, F., & Nanavaty-Dahl, J. (2009). Set up remote workers to thrive. *MIT Sloan Management Review.* Retrieved from http://sloanreview.mit.edu/article/set-up-remote-workers-to-thrive/

41   McCready, A., Lockhart, C., & Sieyes, J. (2001). Telemanaging. *Management Services,* 45(12), 14-16.

42   Clemons, D., & Kroth M. (2011). *Managing the mobile workforce.* New York, NY:McGraw-Hill Companies.

43   Sims, H. P., Faraj, S., & Yun, S. (2009) When should a leader be directive or empowering? How to develop your own situational theory of leadership. *Business Horizons,* 52(2), 149-158. doi:10.1016/j.bushor.2008.10.002

44   Leeman, J. E. (2010). Let's get real about empowering employees. *Industrial Safety & Hygiene News,* 44(12), 18-20.

45   Ibid.

46   Bennis, W. (1991). Learning some basic truisms about leadership. *National Forum.* 71(1), 12-15.

47 Peters, P., den Dulk, L., & De Ruijter, J. (2010). Equality, diversity and inclusion: An international journal. *Emerald Article,* 29(5) 517-531. doi:10.1108/0261015011052799

48 Ibid.

49 Leonard, B. (2011, June). Managing virtual teams. *HR Magazine,* 39-42.

50 Solomon, C. M. (2000, May). Don't forget your telecommuters. *Workforce,* 56-61.

51 Elsbach, K. D, & Cable, D. M. (2012). Why showing your face at work matters. *MIT Sloan Management Review.* 53(4). Retrieved from http://sloanreview.mit.edu/article/why-showing-your-face-at-work-matters/

52 Ibid.

53 Chronos Consulting. (2011). *The state of virtual team utilization in the 21st century: A research survey.* Retrieved from http://www.chronosconsulting.org/dl/Virtual-Teams-Utilization-Research-Survey-Sep-1-2011.pdf

54 Roy, S. R. (2012). Digital mastery: The skills needed for effective virtual leadership. *International Journal of e-Collaboration,* 8(3), 56-66.

55 Ibid.

56 Snyder, K. (2012). Enhancing telework—A guide to virtual leadership. *The Public Manager.* Retrieved from http://www.

astd.org/Publications/Magazines/The-Public-Manager/
Archives/2012/Spring/Enhancing-Telework-a-Guide-to-
Virtual-Leadership

57 Offstein, E. H., & Morwock, J. M. (2009). *Making telework
work.* Boston, MASS: Davies-Black.

58 Maruyama, T., & Tietze, S. (2012). From anxiety to assurance: Concerns and outcomes of telework. *Emerald.* 41(4),
450-469. doi:10.1108/00483481211229375

59 Chronos Consulting. (2011). *The state of virtual team
utilization in the 21st century: A research survey.* Retrieved
from http://www.chronosconsulting.org/dl/Virtual-Teams-
Utilization-Research-Survey-Sep-1-2011.pdf

60 Yu, S. (2008, December). How to make teleworking work:
Widespread adoption of telecommuting programs is often
hindered by non-technical factors. *Communication News,*
30-32.

61 Appelbaum, E., & Milkman, R. (2006). Achieving a work-
able balance: New Jersey employers' experiences managing
employee leaves and turnover. *Center for Women and Work.*
New York: Rutgers University. Retrieved from http://www.
mobilityagenda.org /achieve.pdf?attredirects=0

62 Snyder, K. (2012). Enhancing telework—A guide to virtual
leadership. *The Public Manager.* Retrieved from http://www.
astd.org/Publications/Magazines/The-Public-Manager/
Archives/2012/Spring/Enhancing-Telework-a-Guide-to-
Virtual-Leadership

63 Mulki, J., Nardhi, F., Laddek, F., & Nanavaty-Dahl, J. (2009). Set up remote workers to thrive. *MIT Sloan Management Review.* Retrieved from http://sloanreview.mit.edu/ article/set-up-remote-workers-to-thrive/

64 Cole, A. (2012, May 30). Retaining young feds takes finesse. *Federal Computer Week,* 15.

65 Almer, E. D., & Kaplan, S. E. (2002). The effects of flexible work arrangements on stressors, burnout, and behavioral job outcomes in public accounting. *Behavior Research in Accounting,* 14(1), 1-34. doi:10.2308/bria.2002.14.1.1

66 Sharit, J., Czaja, S. J., Hernandez, M. A., & Nair, S. N. (2009). The employability of older workers as teleworkers: An appraisal of issues and an empirical study. *Journal of Human Factors in Ergonomics & Manufacturing,* 19(5), 457-477.

67 Almer, E. D., & Kaplan, S. E. (2002). The effects of flexible work arrangements on stressors, burnout, and behavioral job outcomes in public accounting. *Behavior Research in Accounting,* 14(1), 1-34. doi:10.2308/bria.2002.14.1.1

68 Hamel, G. (2012). *What Matters Now.* San Francisco, CA: Jossey-Bass.

69 Matos, (2015). Workflex and Telework Guide: Everyone's Guide to Working Anywhere. *Families and Work Institute.* http://www.whenworkworks.org/downloads/workflex-and-telework-guide.pdf

70   Ibid.

71   Ibid.

72   National Federation of Independent Business. (n.d.). *State by State Comparison of Worker's Compensation Laws.* Retrieved September 17, 2012 from http://www.nfib.com/legal-center/compliance-resource-center/compliance-resource-item/cmsid/57181

73   Kratz, G. (2016). 6 Telecommuting Legal Issues for Employers to Consider. *Flexijobs.* https://www.flexjobs.com/employer-blog/telecommuting-legal-issues/

74   Fjermestad, J. (2009, March). Virtual leadership for a virtual workforce. *Chief Learning Officer,* 36-39.

75   Diversify. (2013). *Understanding the Filipino Culture.* https://www.diversifyoss.com/newsroom/understanding-filipino-culture/

76   Ng, P.S. (2011). 2011 Cultural Intelligence and Collective Efficacy in Virtual Team Effectiveness Pei See Ng Minnesota State University—Mankato. *CORNERSTONE.* https://cornerstone.lib.mnsu.edu/cgi/viewcontent.cgi?referer=https://www.google.com/&httpsredir=1&article=1163&context=etds

77   Rafter, M. (2011, November). Out of site. *Benefits Magazine,* 51.

78   Bass, B. M., & Avolio, B. J. (1993). Transformational leadership and organizational culture. *Public Administration Quarterly*, 17(1), 112-121.

79   Smits, K. (2014). *Intercultural Collaboration in the Workplace: Why Bother?* https://www.linkedin.com/pulse/2014 1017122230-13342609-intercultural-collaboration-in-the-workplace-why-bother/

80   Goman, K. (2016). *None Of Us Is Smarter Than All Of Us: Collaborative Leadership From A To Z Forbes*. https://www.forbes.com/sites/carolkinseygoman/2016/05/01/none-of-us-is-smarter-than-all-of-us-collaborative-leadership-from-a-to-z/#511161fc4ab0

81   Manpower, (n.d.). The world of virtual work facts and statistics [Fact sheet]. Retrieved from http://files.shareholder.com/downloads/MAN/164668571x0x117500/bebbb96d-64a8-4a24-a3ab-1a41eeffb7db/MP_World%20of%20Virtual%20Work%20Facts_Stats_FINAL.pdf

82   Ishida, T. (n.d.). Language Grid: An Infrastructure for Intercultural Collaboration. Department of Social Informatics, Kyoto University Kyoto 606-8501 JAPAN ishida@i.kyoto-u.ac.jp http://mail.langrid.org/publications/06/ishida-saint 2006.pdf

83   Dowling, D. (2013). Global Telecommuting Brings a Host of Issues. *SHRM*. https://www.shrm.org/resourcesandtools/hr-topics/global-hr/pages/global-telecommuting-issues.aspx

84   Ibid.

85   Solomon, C. M. (2000, May). Don't forget your telecom-
     muters. *Workforce,* 56-61.

86   Gibson, J. W., Blackwell, C. W., Dominicis, P., & Dener-
     ath, N. (2002). Telecommuting in the 21ˢᵗ century: Bene-
     fits, issues, and a leadership model which will work. *Jour-
     nal of Leadership & Organizational Studies.* 8, 75-86. doi:
     10.1177/107179190200800407

87   Goman, K. (2016). *None Of Us Is Smarter Than All Of Us:
     Collaborative Leadership From A To Z Forbes.* https://www.
     forbes.com/sites/carolkinseygoman/2016/05/01/none-of-
     us-is-smarter-than-all-of-us-collaborative-leadership-from-
     a-to-z/#511161fc4ab0

88   Digeneo, C. (2018). 47 Online Collaboration Tools to Help
     Your Team Be More Productive. *Time Doctor.* https://biz30.
     timedoctor.com/online-collaboration-tools/

89   Venkatesh, V., & Speier, C. (2000). Creating an effective
     training environment for enhancing telework. *Interna-
     tional Journal of Human-Computer Studies,* 52, 991-1005.
     doi:10.1006/ijhc.1999.0367

90   Fjermestad, J. (2009, March). Virtual leadership for a virtual
     workforce. *Chief Learning Officer,* 36-39.

91   Roy, S. R. (2012). Digital mastery: The skills needed for ef-
     fective virtual leadership. *International Journal of e-Collabo-
     ration,* 8(3), 56-66.

92 Wagner, C. (2004, March/April). Fear and loathing in the virtual workplace. *The Futurist,* 6-7.

93 Whittle, A., & Mueler, F. (2009). 'I could be dead for two weeks and my boss would never know': Telework and the politics of representation. *New Technology, Work and Employment,* 24(2), 131-143.

94 Zhang, S., & Fjermestad, J. (2006). Bridging the gap between traditional leadership theories and virtual team leadership. International Journal of Technology, *Policy and Management,* 6(3), 274-291.

95 Walker, A. (2010, September, 29). Out of sight, out of mind? Managing the teleworker. *Gartner,* G00206935, 1-9.

96 Leonard, B. (2011, June). Managing virtual teams. *HR Magazine,* 39-42.

97 Cordery, J., Soo, C., Kirkman, B., Roses, B., & Mathieu, J. (2009). Leading parallel global virtual teams: Lessons from Alcoa. *Organizational Dynamics,* 38(3), 204-216. doi:10.1016/j.orgdyn.2009.04.002

98 Cordery, J., Soo, C., Kirkman, B., Roses, B., & Mathieu, J. (2009). Leading parallel global virtual teams: Lessons from Alcoa. *Organizational Dynamics,* 38(3), 204-216. doi:10.1016/j.orgdyn.2009.04.002

99 Sims, H. P., Faraj, S., & Yun, S. (2009) When should a leader be directive or empowering? How to develop your own

situational theory of leadership. *Business Horizons,* 52(2), 149-158. doi:10.1016/j.bushor.2008.10.002

100 Bens, I. (2007). The ten essential processes of facilitative leaders. *Global Business & Organizational Excellence,* 26(5), 38-56. doi:10.1002/joe.20163

101 Phillips, A. (2014). Want to Be a Better Leader? Show Employees You Care. *Entrepreneur.* https://www.entrepreneur.com/article/236806

102 Phillips, A. (2014). Want to Be a Better Leader? Show Employees You Care. *Entrepreneur.* https://www.entrepreneur.com/article/236806

103 Patel, S. (2017). The 5 Charisitcs That Make a Charismatic Leader. *Entrepreneur.* https://www.entrepreneur.com/article/297710

104 Phillips, A. (2014). Want to Be a Better Leader? Show Employees You Care. *Entrepreneur.* https://www.entrepreneur.com/article/236806

105 Flelkow, B. (2014). Managers Can Be True Leaders Not Just Taskmasters, *Entrepreneur.* https://www.entrepreneur.com/article/235929

106 Flelkow, B. (2014). Managers Can Be True Leaders Not Just Taskmasters, *Entrepreneur.* https://www.entrepreneur.com/article/235929

107 Clear, F., Dickson, K. (2005). Teleworking Practice in Small and Medium-Sized Firms: Management Style and Worker Autonomy *New Technology, Work and Employment,* 20(3):218-229. https://pdfs.semanticscholar.org/eb87/3eacbf4e86e90c0621 c27592e56417362699.pdf

108 Leonard, B. (2011, June). Managing virtual teams. *HR Magazine,* 39-42.

109 Walker, A. (2010, September, 29). Out of sight, out of mind? Managing the teleworker. *Gartner,* G00206935, 1-9.

110 Walker, A. (2010, September, 29). Out of sight, out of mind? Managing the teleworker. *Gartner,* G00206935, 1-9.

111 Cole, A. (2012, May 30). Retaining young feds takes finesse. *Federal Computer Week,* 15.

112 Spector, N. (2017). You Snooze, You Lose? The Majority of Americans Wake Up Thinking About Money. *NBC News.* https://www.nbcnews.com/business/consumer/you-snooze-you-lose-majority-americans-wake-thinking-about-money-n800911

113 Kanter, R. M. (2001). Power, leadership, and participatory management. *Theory Into Practice.* 20(4), 219-224

114 Cascio, W., & Shurygailo, S. (2003). E-leadership and virtual teams. *Organizational Dynamics,* 31(4), 362-376.

115 Speagle, A. (2015). The Power of Saying 'Good Morning' to Your Virtual Team. *Collaborative Exchange.* https://www.

pgi.com/blog/2015/08/the-best-morning-routine-for-virtual-team-building/

116 Saunderson, R. (2011). Top 10 Ways to Recognize, Motivate Your Telecommuters. *Incentive Magazine*. http://www.incentivemag.com/article.aspx?id=7255

117 Purvanova, R. K., & Bono, J. E. (2009). Transformation leadership in context: Face-to-face and virtual teams. *The Leadership Quarterly*, 20(2009), 343-357. doi:10.1016/j.leaqua.2009.03.004

118 Robbins, S.P. & Judge, T.A. (2011). Organizational Behavior. *Saddle River*, N.J.: Prentice Hall.

119 Simic, I. (1999). Transformational leadership—The key to successful management of transformational organizational changes. *Facta Universitatis: Economics and Organization*, 1(6), 49-55.

120 Morris, S. (2008). Virtual team working: Making it happen. *Industrial and Commercial Training*, 40(3), 129-133. doi:10.1108/00197850810868812

121 Fjermestad, J. (2009, March). Virtual leadership for a virtual workforce. *Chief Learning Officer*, 36-39.

122 Patel, S. (2017). The 5 Charisitcs That Make a Charismatic Leader. *Entrepreneur*. https://www.entrepreneur.com/article/297710

123 Ibid.

124 Morris, S. (2008). Virtual team working: Making it happen. *Industrial and Commercial Training*, 40(3), 129-133. doi:10.1108/0019785081086812

125 Walinskas, K. (2012). Telework and virtual team leadership. *Business Know How*. Retrieved from http://www.businessknowhow.com/manage/telework.htm

126 Walker, A. (2010, September, 29). Out of sight, out of mind? Managing the teleworker. *Gartner*, G00206935, 1-9.

127 Reed, R. (2017). Charm Isn't Elusive, Train Yourself to Become *Magnetic*. https://www.theguardian.com/small-business-network/2017/mar/03/charisma-train-yourself-magnetic-entrepreneurs-win-customers

128 Fonner, K. L. (2012). *Overcommunication causes stress for teleworkers*. Retrieved from http://www.astd.org/Publications/Magazines/TD/TD-Archive/2012/09/ Overcommunication-Causes-Stress-for-Teleworkers

ABOUT THE AUTHOR

Founder of Sommét Enterprises, LLC, Dr. Ann Gladys is a dynamic speaker, author, and experienced organizational development professional specializing in productivity and leadership. Dr. Gladys has worked with organizations crossing Information Technology, Academia, and Non-Profits and leverages this triangular experience to create positive growth in all three arenas.

Dr. Gladys is a thought leader and pioneer in the Virtual Workspace. She is the author of published journal articles, and has created the tools and assessments to identify and develop leaders to succeed in managing virtual employees (aka teleworkers).

Dr. Gladys has taught in three doctoral programs at various

universities in Ph.D., Ed.D., and, DBA programs. Her courses span topics from Strategic Leadership, Research, Global Leadership, and Inferential Statistics.

Creating, spotlighting, and teaching professional and organizational entities and positioning them for growth and success is what Ann has done throughout her career. This aligns with her goals and objectives for developing leaders and educating students in the fields of business and leadership. Ann's work reflects a personal belief system where the individual is valued, respected, trusted, and encouraged.

LEADERSHIP DEVELOPMENT PROGRAMS

For additional information concerning customized leadership development programs and special topics including:

Invisible Leadership
Leadership Intelligence
Change Management
Cultural Intelligence
Leading through Communication, Trust, and Respect
Emotional Intelligence
Succession Planning
Global Leadership
Personal Leadership and Social Intelligence
Creating Effective Virtual Teams
Time, Technology, and Priority Management
Communicating Effectively and Appropriately in a Virtual
Workspace
Myths and Realities of the Virtual Workspace
Building Trust and Empowering Employees in
a Virtual Work Environment
Delivering Substantial Results as a Virtual Team
Cross-Cultural Training

Conflict Resolution in a Virtual Work Environment
As well as other topics . . .

Please feel free to contact me at:
agladys@sommetenterprises.com
http://www.sommetenterprises.com/

30859172R00091

Made in the USA
San Bernardino, CA
31 March 2019